# ADVANCE PRAISE

"For anyone looking to ratchet down the shouting and ratchet up the solutions in today's society, look no further than Rich's book. Having dedicated his career to community building, Rich understands that people—and their dignity—lie at the heart of strong communities. Rich knows how to heal divides, build bridges, and help all people find greater opportunity, and his experiences weave together a story of hope and purpose that we can all use to build better selves and support the places we call home."

**—BRIAN GALLAGHER,** President and CEO, United Way Worldwide

"*Stepping Forward* is a profound and inspiring book by one of our leading organizers. Blending memoir, reporting, and razor-sharp, strategic analysis of how social change happens, Rich Harwood offers an unforgettable account of what it means to connect, engage, and transform the world. It's a powerful call to action, a necessary read for these difficult times."

**—ERIC KLINENBERG,** Professor of Sociology at New York University and author of *Palaces for the People: How Social Infrastructure Can Help Fight Inequality, Polarization, and the Decline of Civic Life*

"Reflecting on thirty years of transformational work in the field, Rich Harwood presents a critical case of people-centered service, which keeps intact human dignity, connection, and individualism—a message especially important in this time when mistrust and divisions dominate the headlines. He shares poignant lessons from his journey, laying a compelling framework to guide us forward, to a hopeful future."

**—MICHELE NUNN,** President and CEO, CARE USA

"*Stepping Forward* thunders with optimism amid an America overwhelmed with worry. Decades of work in communities large and small informs Harwood's unique perspective on an America that has lost its way. Eschewing mere diagnosis, Rich Harwood teaches us how to bind our cultural wounds, embrace our shared humanity, and, in so doing, remake our Republic. In an America where too many have weaponized difference for their own ends, *Stepping Forward* is a well-timed act of civic faith, reminding us that none are exempt, as Senator Edward M. Kennedy said, 'from the common obligation to give of ourselves.'"

—**MELODY BARNES,** Co-Director, Democracy Initiative, University of Virginia and former Director, White House Domestic Policy Council (2009–20012)

"Many people are distressed by today's bitter divisiveness and feel powerless to affect the forces shaping their lives. Rich offers up a set of simple but profound insights for making a difference, drawn from a lifetime of reflection and working in communities around the country. *Stepping Forward* is a powerful and timely book."

—**DAVID MATHEWS,** President, Kettering Foundation

"Richard Harwood has written a practical book about dreams. This is no oxymoron. In *Stepping Forward*, Harwood shows how community transformation involves unlocking personal aspirations and linking them to our innate desire to be part of something larger than ourselves. He captures the spiritual essence of what it has meant in our past to be American, inviting each one of us to be part of that great journey. It is therefore really a book about the human soul. The very language of the book tells it all: covenant, resilience, dignity, loyalty, faith, and love. When we discover each other's deep humanness, we forge bonds that enable us to create our future together. Rich Harwood shows us how."

—**RABBI DANIEL G. ZEMEL,** Temple Micah, Washington, DC

"*Stepping Forward* offers thoughtful guidance about one of the most important tasks facing our country: building the civic infrastructure of communities to help them solve problems, cross divides, and find common ground. Through inspiring stories of communities like Sandy Hook, Mobile, Battle Creek, Youngstown, and more, this book proves one of the key principles it offers: Communities gain hope by seeing others."

**—HILARY PENNINGTON,** Executive Vice President for Program, Ford Foundation

"In *Stepping Forward* Richard Harwood, divinely inspired and masterfully, elevates our thinking toward various and pressing challenges we face in our communities. He accomplishes this while simultaneously offering pragmatic approaches for a path forward. I have spent considerable time in many of the places that Rich highlights, and I've seen and experienced some of his work firsthand. The results are real. Rich is answering a clarion call from our nation's hardest hit communities. Fortified with the knowledge and inspiration from this book, we should all now proceed to join him."

**—JAY WILLIAMS,** President and CEO, Hartford Foundation for Public Giving; former Mayor of Youngstown, Ohio; and Assistant Secretary of Commerce in the Obama Administration

"In a time when people feel hopeless and helpless, Harwood offers practical and spiritually inspiring advice about how community builders can learn to find common ground and create a civic culture, not just carry out a civic program. A profound aspect of this book is its recognition of the hunger for human dignity and for the ability to shape our own lives."

**—BETTY SUE FLOWERS,** Professor Emeritus, University of Texas at Austin and former Director, Lyndon B. Johnson Presidential Library

"*Stepping Forward* is a moving account of local communities dealing with some of the key questions that often arise in the process of creating the change they so desire. In his reflection, Richard Harwood draws inspiration from the Biblical Moses in his famous response 'Here I am.' During these polarized times, Richard is active in communities that desperately need to turn outward. A central message running throughout the book provides us with a renewed sense of hope—by building upon shared values rather than emphasizing divisions, we can make important progress."

**—WILLICE ONYANGO,** Executive Director, The Youth Cafe, Kenya

"Rich Harwood calls us back to a pragmatic American idealism. His perspective is unique and timely. Read *Stepping Forward* and rediscover your individual purpose and how we can shape our shared future, together."

**—SHIRLEY SAGAWA,** CEO, Service Year

# STEPPING FORWARD

## A POSITIVE, PRACTICAL PATH
## TO TRANSFORM OUR
## COMMUNITIES AND OUR LIVES

## Richard C. Harwood

GREENLEAF
BOOK GROUP PRESS

Published by Greenleaf Book Group Press
Austin, Texas
www.gbgpress.com

Distributed by Greenleaf Book Group

For ordering information or special discounts for bulk purchases, please contact Greenleaf Book Group at PO Box 91869, Austin, TX 78709, 512.891.6100.

Design and composition by Greenleaf Book Group and Sheila Parr
Cover design by Greenleaf Book Group and Sheila Parr

Publisher's Cataloging-in-Publication data is available.

Print ISBN: 978-1-62634-676-5

eBook ISBN: 978-1-62634-677-2

Part of the Tree Neutral® program, which offsets the number of trees consumed in the production and printing of this book by taking proactive steps, such as planting trees in direct proportion to the number of trees used: www.treeneutral.com

TreeNeutral®

Printed in the United States of America on acid-free paper

19 20 21 22 23 24    10 9 8 7 6 5 4 3 2 1

First Edition

*To my wife Jackie—you have helped me step forward*
*in more ways than I can count.*

"People say, what good can one person do?

What is the sense of our small effort?"

These are the words of Dorothy Day.

She went on to say, "They cannot see that

we must lay one brick at a time,

take one step at a time."[1]

She believed that our individual actions

ripple out far beyond our imagination

in all directions. And so we must maintain

our sense of hope. There's much work to do.

These words guided me as I

wrote this book, and for years they have

inspired me to step forward.

---

1   Dorothy Day, *Loaves and Fishes: The Inspiring Story of the Catholic Worker Movement* (Maryknoll, New York: Orbis, 2003): 176.

# CONTENTS

# ACKNOWLEDGMENTS

I have been thinking about writing this book for a number of years, and I am grateful to a whole host of people who have helped me make it happen.

Neil Richardson brought Walt Whitman and various American philosophers into much sharper focus for me and encouraged me to place our ideas and work at The Harwood Institute for Public Innovation in a larger historical context. It was with Neil that I began in earnest my conversations about civic faith.

My friends at the Kettering Foundation have for 30 years actively supported my work on these ideas; I am especially indebted to its president, David Mathews.

I am enormously grateful to Rabbi Danny Zemel, who has helped me to express my faith and who has shown his faith in me. And to Hawaii State Senator Les Ihara, who has consistently encouraged me to articulate my thoughts.

Mike Wood helped me shape many of these ideas during our two stints of working together; as have many Harwood Institute coaches I have worked hand-in-hand with over many years, including Karen Aldridge-Eason, Bill Booth, Marla Crockett, Jan Elliott, Cheryl Gorman, David Moore, Carlton Sears, Susan Taylor Simpson, and Brian Smith.

As I was pulling ideas together and writing the manuscript, Grady Lenkin, my special assistant at the time, read numerous drafts, gave me wonderful feedback, and offered steadfast encouragement. Christine Kim, our inaugural studio associate at The Harwood Institute, also provided keen insights, always pushing for more clarity and concreteness. And I am appreciative of the gentle nudges from our studio associate Sarah Goodwin Thiel. David Moore and Brad Rourke, two colleagues, and even better friends, provided invaluable guidance.

I appreciate all that Miranda Klugesherz, Colleen Bowman, Paige DeLoach, and Damien Conners have done in working with Greenleaf Book Group and developing and implementing the plans to promote this book. It's a team effort.

The folks at Greenleaf have been a pleasure to work with. My editor, Lindsey Clark, guided me through my final drafts and made this book stronger.

This book is a product of my life. And so I want to offer a special heartfelt thanks to my dad and mom, to my brother and sister, and to my wife and kids. None of us go it alone—thanks for being on the journey with me.

# A Reflection

# HERE I AM

For as long as I can remember, my favorite words in the Bible have been *Here I am*. These three tiny words hold huge meaning not only for people of religious faith but also for those of us concerned about our shared ability to create the kinds of communities and lives we want. At this moment in America, these three words call on us to engage with one another—to take greater responsibility for where we are and who we can become.

The words *Here I am* appear repeatedly throughout the Bible—from Abraham to Samuel to Isaiah, and elsewhere. But the story this phrase reminds me of most involves Moses. Standing before the burning bush, at first trembling and hiding his face, he ultimately answers God's call by saying, "Here I am."

In that moment, Moses—who doubts his capabilities, his strength, his own voice, his identity—does something that is desperately needed in our communities and our country today. In his moment of trial, Moses makes himself visible. He does not hide. He does not turn away. He does not seek cover. He makes an active choice to be present.

Then, God gives him a great task: Go to the mighty Egyptian pharaoh and demand the release of the Israelites from the bonds of slavery. But in the face of this task, Moses hesitates. He asks God, "Who am I?" Once more, his self-doubt is palpable. He is filled with confusion. He thinks he is unworthy. But, as we know, Moses proves otherwise. He heeds the call.

He steps forward. He acts. What are the implications of Moses' words and actions for each of us today? Indeed, what about us? Will we act?

At the burning bush, Moses is asked to take an action that none of us will be called to do, but we can still learn from his story. When he hears the call, he personally makes an active choice. He chooses to step forward. He engages. He shows his face.

He *accounts* for himself too. There is something uniquely powerful in this personal act. In our society, *accountability* often means following laws, achieving certain measurable goals, or making formal reports. What I love about the story of Moses and the burning bush is that the idea of accounting for oneself takes on a much larger, deeper meaning. It asks each of us to assume full responsibility for who we can become and what we must do. It summons us to measure ourselves based on whether we are living up to the pledges and promises we have made to ourselves and to others. This is not about a typical professional accountability. It is a covenant we make with one another about the kind of world we seek to create together.

So, as you read this book, I ask you to keep in mind the following questions. These are questions people ask me all the time as I work with them in their communities:

- How can I come together with others to truly make a difference?
- How do I make the kinds of leaps in my life that will enable me to have the impact I seek in my community and elsewhere?
- How can my engagement reflect the best in myself and in others?
- How can I unleash a greater sense of shared responsibility in my community and in my work?
- How do I find the courage and humility to take such a path?

There are times when I have fears and self-doubts about my own capabilities. We all do. We often believe that someone else is more equipped, better prepared, or more articulate for what needs to be said and done. We fear the unknown. At times we fear the other. We step back when people's anger and grievances turn into words and emotions we find hurtful and uncomfortable.

But we must take the lesson of Moses and make ourselves visible. We must be present, alive, and awake in this moment. We must be *here*. This requires each of us to face our challenges head-on if we are to tackle the challenges our society confronts.

We need not know on our own all the answers to these challenges—none of us can. Nor must we go it alone. Positive change never happens in that way.

Instead, we must simply keep these three tiny words in mind: *Here I am.*

# Introduction

# AWAKEN

"He's a Lemon."

That's how my doctors described me to my mom when I was just a few years old, after I was diagnosed with cystic fibrosis. In the early 1960s, that was a death sentence. Much of my youth and early adulthood was spent in hospital beds. I can still vividly recall all the doctors, nurses, and specialists routinely surrounding my bed, talking to one another but almost never talking to me.

I was only spoken to when I was being admitted to hospitals. Then, they asked questions, and lots of them. The triage nurses would run down their lists of questions in a seemingly random quest to diagnose what ailed me. I say random because the questions always felt irrelevant. They had little to do with how I was really feeling, where my pain was coming from, the desperate relief I sought, or the deep fears I held. At those times, I was an object caught up in an assembly line that produced a number to be printed on my plastic wristband. I was accurately identified and could be incessantly tracked, and I never felt more lost than at those times. I can still feel the endless medical tests that invaded every part of my body, producing endless humiliation.

My fevers regularly hit 106 degrees. My chills made me tremble uncontrollably. I was force-fed medication I could never keep down. I hallucinated for hours on end, spinning recklessly around my room. I can still hear my mom routinely walking away from my bedroom at night, crying out to my dad, "He's sick again," and the overwhelming shame that rushed through me because I was pulling my family down once more.

To make the craziness stop at night, I invented a ritual of counting the second hand on my clock—one second after another, one minute after another, one hour after another. Each night, I would painstakingly follow this ritual, until I willed myself to the morning light. Then I would no longer be alone in the dark. I had another shot at another day.

I travel now for a living. To my friends, even my family, my travel is thought to be fun, exciting, taking me to new places. To me, it invariably transports me back to an old place. When I open my hotel room door, the sterile, cookie-cutter rooms remind me of a hospital room, triggering more nights of terror.

Until some years ago, when I stayed in hotels, I would sleep in my clothes and turn on every light that I could find, leaving them on all night. Interminably exhausted in the morning, I would somehow make my way through the day, only for another round to begin anew as the dark would come calling out my name.

Throughout my childhood and early adulthood, I was shuffled from one doctor to the next. As months and years passed, different doctors had a different take on what was wrong with me. Each one eventually labeled me with a different diagnosis. And while my doctors diligently tried to fix me, I privately vowed to myself to keep moving forward and to never look back.

My goal was to defy them, and I did. I excelled at sports, at school, and in extracurricular activities throughout my childhood, high school, at Skidmore College, and in graduate school at Princeton University. Because of my difficulties as a child, I felt compelled to ensure that every individual has the opportunity to fulfill their God-given potential and to contribute to the greater good. I worked on 20 political campaigns by the time I was 23 years old. Afterward, I joined two nonprofits that did exhilarating work. Then, at 27 years old, I founded what is now known as The Harwood Institute for Public Innovation.

To this day, no one has been able to explain to me why I was able to outrun my initial death sentence. But here's what I do know for certain. I learned firsthand what it is like to have my dignity stripped from me, what it is to feel invisible and not have a voice, what it means to believe that tomorrow will not be better than today, what it's like to live in constant limbo, not knowing the status of my future or if I would even have one. I was chewed up and spit out by a health care system that pledged to heal me. I was repeatedly made false promises that things would get better by those closest to me. I saw my parents stretched to their absolute limits, and then some.

I also know that part of the reason I did not succumb to fear and despair was because of three wise men that rescued me by playing integral parts in my upbringing. First, there was Ray Rivers who coached me in youth basketball and baseball for years. Some might say he came from the other side of the tracks. He was a laborer at my hometown's Saratoga Race Course. He showed me that despite my illness, in spite of all my anxieties, I could exert myself physically and achieve success in sports and in school—and ultimately in life. Mr. Rivers taught me it was okay to hope.

There was also Jack Petker, who lived a few blocks from my childhood home on leafy Madison Avenue. He was an engineer and a highly respected member of my local synagogue. On weekends, he would take me to do projects at Temple Sinai to fix electrical problems, making me climb the ladder up into the ceiling. In those moments, my legs would tremble from my fear of heights and not knowing what to do. Yet he gently pushed me with the insistence of a drill sergeant and the patience of a saint. I realize now that he was helping me see that I could rise up over my fears and reach my potential.

Then there was my next-door neighbor Jack Brundidge, who worked at the local General Mills assembly plant where Cheerios and other breakfast cereals were packaged. Mr. Brundidge was a proud gun owner. Every night he drank Pabst Blue Ribbon on his tiny backyard patio. In his woodshop, he taught me I could build things with my own hands.

From these three men, I learned what dignity felt like. To finally believe I had a voice. To be seen and heard. I learned that the labels we assign to people are often misleading, even dead wrong. Each person has hidden gifts, talents, and a relentless power for good within them. And while experts are essential in our search to solve hard problems, such expertise often comes from the least expected places.

The maladies I suffered as a child and young adult are not so different from the maladies that our communities and society suffer from now. Too many people feel they have lost their own sense of dignity. Often, people who have good intentions, but who know far too little about the aspirations of the people and communities they are trying to help, impose misguided solutions. Far too many Americans have lost faith in our leaders and institutions because of repeated unfulfilled promises. Our politics and public discourse have become so contentious and convoluted that people can no longer see and hear themselves in it.

I wrote this book for those of us who believe we must reject the current frustration, gridlock, and cynicism of our times; who know none of us can go it alone; who believe we can do better; and who want to work with others to get things done, together.

My hope is that you're reading this book because you know that despite the uphill battle we face, it is still worth persevering to make tomorrow better than today—for everyone.

This book lays out a new path—a more hopeful path. Where we rediscover what we share in common and actively build upon it. Where we value and draw upon the wherewithal, know-how, and wisdom we already have to improve our lives and communities. Where we bring a greater sense of purpose and meaning back into our own individual lives.

I am not offering some utopian vision. I don't have time for more false pledges and promises. I've had my personal fill. And I'm sure you have too. What I am proposing is real and practical. But here's the thing: We must create it together. We need to see ourselves as co-creators of our own lives and communities.

This book is rooted in my larger civic faith, which has grown and been shaped over the years through my professional and personal experiences. It informs all I do, sits at the core of all my efforts, and echoes throughout these pages.

At the heart of this civic faith are people. People must always be at the center of what we do—their lives, what matters to them, their aspirations. People's dignity is paramount to this. So too is the need to recognize people's desire to find ways to express their agency, together—to bring about change in their own lives and in our collective lives. People are often left out, overlooked, pushed aside, or rendered inconsequential. Their dignity denied. We must fix this.

This civic faith is rooted in the belief in people's innate capabilities to shape their own lives and the lives of those in their communities. That under the right conditions, we can transcend our vital self-interests to forge a stronger common good—that each of us longs to be part of something larger than ourselves. This doesn't mean we will agree on everything or always like one another. But we do have the capabilities to figure out what we do share and work on that together.

Also vital to this civic faith is the centrality of hope in our lives. More than anything, people want a sense of possibility and hope—to believe that tomorrow can be better than today. Through our words and actions, we each get to choose whether we engender authentic hope or false hope. It is a choice that each of us gets to make and that no one can take from us. We must know that false hope pushes people away and gives rise to cynicism, fear, and mistrust; authentic hope, on the other hand, is the fuel we need to put one foot in front of the other and take action that will strengthen communities and transform lives.

At the essence of this civic faith is the conviction that community is a common enterprise. We cannot create the kind of shared lives we seek on our own. Yes, the idea of individualism is a hallmark of American society; I subscribe fervently to it. But so, too, is the fact that we make our communities and country great by building them together. In these times, when we can feel isolated and alone, we must continually remind ourselves of this enduring truth that community is made by us.

And at the core of this civic faith sits a covenant—a *civic* covenant. We are in relationship with one another—that is the only way a shared society works. Programs, processes, and technical approaches are all important to implementing ideas and initiatives. But nothing can substitute for the relational nature of community and society—the inherent need to forge productive relationships with one another, nurture them, pay attention to them, and make them vibrant and alive.

With this backdrop in mind, I want to give you a road map for what I think our challenges are and what I think we can do as individuals and communities to help fix these problems.

There are four key forces at work around us, serving to undermine our politics, separate us from one another, foster mistrust, and disorient us. These forces have been emerging over recent decades—they are not new. They present us with challenges, but I believe we can overcome them.

What we must do to counter the current environment and create a more hopeful path is to focus on the things we share and can build together. And each of us must lean into our own lives and make choices to find the things we share with others and gain greater meaning and purpose in our own life.

The book draws on my over 30 years of working to strengthen communities, solve problems, and improve people's lives. My work has now spread to all 50 US states and is being used in over 40 countries.

I have personally toiled in some of the hardest-hit communities, working with inspiring local leaders to take on their most pressing challenges—including in Flint, Michigan; Youngstown, Ohio; the Mississippi Delta; Las Vegas; and Mobile, Alabama.

I have teamed up with the largest nonprofit organizations in the world to help them become more relevant to people's lives and more impactful in what they do, including United Way Worldwide, AARP, Goodwill Industries International, the American Library Association, and the Corporation for Public Broadcasting.

My efforts have been supported by some of the best-known foundations around the globe, including the Bill & Melinda Gates Foundation, The Pew Charitable Trusts, the Charles Stewart Mott Foundation, the Knight Foundation, the Omidyar Network, and the Kettering Foundation, among others.

I have been called to help communities move forward after some of the toughest and saddest challenges our society can confront, including the massacre at Sandy Hook Elementary School in Newtown, Connecticut.

Everything here has been road-tested, time-tested, and market-tested. It works.

I have also experienced my own share of failures and heartbreaks along the way. I have messed up and screwed up. I have been enormously humbled by these mistakes. At times, they have filled me with self-doubt about my own capabilities. But these mistakes have taught me as much as any of my successes. They have relentlessly driven me to innovate each and every day to find better answers to our society's ills and to help people reach their aspirations for their lives and communities.

Laying in a hospital bed for so long, feeling invisible, my dignity shattered, made me want to get up, get moving, and get something done. I hope this book inspires you to join me.

Each of us will need to reach within and beyond ourselves to do this to create the kinds of lives and communities we seek.

# Part I

# TRAPPED

# NOISE AND CONFUSION

On December 14, 2012, a 20-year-old gunman named Adam Lanza walked into the Sandy Hook Elementary School in Newtown, Connecticut, massacring 20 first graders and 6 adults. It was an unthinkable tragedy that rocked Newtown and the nation. President Barack Obama said it was the most difficult day of his presidency.

Just weeks after the shooting, I received a phone call from Patricia Llodra, Newtown's first selectman, the town's chief executive. She asked if I'd design and lead the process by which the community would decide what to do with the elementary school building where the tragedy occurred.

I weighed the decision for days. My initial instinct was to call Pat back and decline. The task seemed overwhelming. How would I even go about it? There was no road map, no known process for a situation like this. I was filled with self-doubt.

But when I really thought about it, I felt I had little choice. I had to step forward. I was not powerless to act. I had worked extensively with other severely hit communities, and I knew instinctively that this experience would draw upon lessons and sensitivities I had gained from my own childhood traumas. So I accepted. And I learned very quickly just how challenging it would be. This was a discussion about the future of a school building, but it was also about so much more. Could the Newtown community pivot from trauma and despair to healing and hope?

Newtown provides a window into what we, as people and communities, are capable of under the worst conditions. It shows that we can rise above our instincts and impulses to separate from one another, to go it alone, to cast aspersions of blame, and to doubt one another's motivations. We can take hope from Newtown.

This story also illustrates a sharp juxtaposition to where we are as a nation today. In our lives and communities, various forces are working against us—many that we created ourselves—and we must understand these forces if we wish to find a more hopeful path.

## A BIG DECISION

Focusing on the future of the school building would be the first significant public decision the Newtown community would have to make after the shooting. Many residents argued that it was too soon to hold this discussion. The wounds were still too raw, and they needed more time to let things settle. This debate went back and forth until Pat, who I would come to know as the *best* public leader I have ever worked with, made the choice to move forward.

She appointed a 28-member task force made up of individuals from four different town-governing boards, including the town commission, the board of education, the finance commission, and the parks commission. The task force was to decide whether to renovate the existing school, rebuild on the same site, or start fresh on a new property.

I came on board to guide the task force in early February. We had until May to make a decision due to various timelines, including that of the state legislature, which needed to know if it had to appropriate any new dollars for the school project. During that time, the task force evaluated some 40 alternatives and weighed the pros and cons of their choices and the trade-offs of each option.

I feared the setup was a recipe for political disaster. Long-standing tensions riled the governing boards. The community was divided not only on whether to hold this discussion but also there was disagreement about what to do with the school building. Should it remain or be torn down?

Adding fuel to this highly combustible situation were the national and state political figures, organized interest groups, and news media swarming all over the community. Political grandstanding, positioning, posturing, and gridlock were all in the offing.

## FINDING OUR WAY

I remember vividly the first day I met Pat in person. It was in the conference room of her small office suite. About a dozen other community leaders, some of whom would later serve on the task force, were also present. At issue was how to shape the task force goals, the overall process, and its individual meetings.

People disagreed about what to do. Frustrations ran high. I wrestled with whether this group was actually ready to take on such an emotionally charged discussion. Were the trauma and despair just too great to deal with? Could people be flexible enough to hear one another? Could I devise an approach and strategy that could work given the level of trauma?

I also needed to find a way to earn Pat's trust, which required a leap of faith on her part to entrust me to guide this process. Plus, by the time of this first meeting, I had developed fairly strong views on how the process should unfold. She pressed me hard that day—and every day after that.

I also remember the first time I met the task force members. It happened literally minutes before our initial public meeting was called to order. All the members were positioned behind the formal task force table at their appointed places. I went up to each one, extending my hand out across the table to introduce myself. Some thought the community needed my help; others did not.

Each task force meeting was held in public in the city council chamber. Families of victims and survivors, Sandy Hook teachers, local businesspeople, and community residents attended the meetings, and they were covered by a barrage of media, including *The Wall Street Journal*, *The New York Times*, *USA Today*, CNN, numerous New York City radio stations, and local media.

As I said, there was no blueprint for how to design and lead such a process. So at the first meeting, I laid out three guideposts for the task force and community. I made clear the basic steps we would follow. Because this was unchartered territory, I presented a clear plan for how we would move forward. People needed to feel a sense of security that they were in safe hands. I then told people that, notwithstanding our timeline, nothing would be rushed. We must be willing to return time and again to issues we once thought we had resolved.

Finally, I named out loud what I suspect many people were already thinking. Even if we reach an agreement on what to do, there's no reason to believe any one of us will feel good about it. How could we? There is no good solution for a situation like this.

Thus amid all the differences, people's individual pain, the community's suffering, and the enormous potential for division, my job was to guide the community to work through their emotions, identify their shared values, and reach a common decision.

## THE LETTER

After months of deliberation, the task force was ready to make a decision. On the day we had planned to decide on the school's future, *The Wall Street Journal* and various other news outlets ran articles announcing the final task force meeting. The process was finally coming to a close.

That morning, as I was reading the news accounts, I received a phone call telling me that a group of 30 or so Sandy Hook Elementary School teachers had just released a public letter declaring that under no conditions would they go back to the school. The question was what to do in response to the letter.

All of our meetings thus far had been held in public. Absolute transparency was a central operating principle of the task force. After flying from my home outside Washington, DC, to Newtown later that day, I met with Pat and we decided to make an exception to our rule. The teachers needed to be heard.

That evening would be the only private meeting we would hold throughout the entire process. We chose to go into the closed session because of the enormous stress and strain the teachers had experienced, and because we wanted them to feel they could fully and openly express themselves without the media and others looking on. Just as the public task force session was set to begin, we cleared the standing-room-only crowd of hundreds of residents and scores of news media and invited the teachers to speak with the task force.

The only people left in the room were the task force members, the teachers, a couple of mental health professionals, and myself. One teacher after another told their stories of hiding students in bathroom stalls and supply closets, hearing gunshots echo throughout the building, and watching loved ones lose their lives. They pleaded with the task force not to have them return to the school building.

As we listened to the teachers tell their stories, I closely watched Pat: no posturing, no speeches, no demands, not even a gentle attempt to reverse the letter. Sitting across the room from the teachers, I could feel her embrace their sorrow and give them the confidence that, no matter what, she would be there for them. Hers was not a political response. It was an act of pure humanity. After each of the teachers got to say what was in their hearts and on their minds, we took a break.

When we reconvened, we invited the rest of the public back in. Townspeople and news media refilled the room, awaiting the final decision. Once the meeting began again, I stood among the restless crowd and announced that no decision would be made that night. The session with the teachers had left too many task force members emotionally shaken. As I said that evening and in media interviews that followed, the closer you get to a final decision about something so important and emotional, the more the implications and consequences of such a decision make themselves clear. This was the ultimate example.

During that tumultuous night, I led the task force members in a discussion about a variety of outstanding issues, save the final decision. We set another time to meet in two weeks. At the end of the meeting, I implored them not to become isolated in the intervening time before our next meeting.

During these two weeks, I told them that their most important tasks were to seek out fellow task force members to talk to, to find other community members and explore their views with them, and to work through the emotions and choices at hand. This was all in hopes of coming to terms themselves with moving forward.

I reminded them that there was always the option of calling off the decision entirely.

## STEPPING FORWARD, GENTLY

When we reconvened for what would be our last meeting, I began by asking the task force members what they had been thinking about over the prior two weeks. One by one, they talked about their conflicting emotions.

One individual who had expressed certitude about what we should do throughout the entire process—at times wondering aloud why we had to talk so much about the ins and outs of the choices we faced—said that he was now confused and scared and no longer sure about what to do.

As different task force members spoke, I remember another member in particular, Laura, sitting to my right. I had met Laura in Pat's conference room on my initial visit to Newtown. She had always been warm and friendly and supportive of my efforts. But that night she was subdued and quiet and withdrawn. She appeared to have something she wanted to say, but she nodded me off each time I motioned to her to go ahead.

Finally, she raised her hand, and when I nodded to her to speak, she gently sat up in her chair. She leaned her elbows on the table, and then, in a low voice, said that she had been thinking a lot about the process, our discussions, the community, the tragedy—and she uttered this handful of words that I will never forget: "We must move on as best we can."

For the next three hours, the task force debated what to do. Clear divisions existed. We seemed destined for gridlock. I kept working the group through areas where they already had reached agreement, seeking to help people to see old arguments anew, discover new options, and come to terms with various trade-offs.

After three incredibly long, tense hours, the conditions eventually emerged. The task force rejected options to move the school to a new site. Instead, the decision was made to raze the current structure, build anew on the current site, and alter the footprint of the building so that it was clear this was a new day.

The vote was unanimous.

## A POWERFUL LESSON

In spite of the emotions and all the difficulties their community faced, the people of Newtown found a way to come together. At times, the process felt like it might fall apart. People became entrenched in their pre-set positions, and some would have a hard time listening to each other. Still, in the end, everyone banded together. Newtown serves as a reminder of our human capacity to overcome obstacles, find what we share in common, and gather our collective will and resources to act, even amid our real differences.

Today, in our country, we are at a crossroads. But rather than come together, our public discourse only coarsens, divisions grow, trust in leaders plummets, and everyone seems to be going their own way. Newtown faced this danger too. And as in Newtown, when everything feels so fragmented, we can feel at a loss. At times, our lives and communities can seem to be spinning out of control. A larger sense of purpose and connection go missing.

During these times, we want to know that we are not stymied or stuck. Despite the odds stacked against us, we want to believe we can make progress. Can tomorrow be better than today?

In order to know where you want to go, you must know where you are. In *Hopeful Imagination*, Walter Brueggemann writes, "the discernment and presentation of the new depend profoundly on knowledge about the old."[1] By "knowledge about the old" he means that you must face reality for what it is.

This was a prerequisite in Newtown. We could not move ahead without first acknowledging the harsh reality of the situation. The same is true when it comes to our personal lives and in our society as a whole. If your goal is to create a different future, then you must face reality. It's that simple—and that difficult.

Today, I see four trends at work in our society that create unyielding noise and confusion that we must face and address before we, like Newtown, can move forward. They are—

1.  Our politics and public life have become about winning at any cost.
2.  Our society is separating at the seams.
3.  More voices make up our public discourse—and many are aggrieved.
4.  There is a profound loss of trust in our leaders and institutions.

Each of these alone, and in combination, makes it hard for us to make sense of where we are and how to get out of this mess.

## Winning at Any Cost

First, our politics has become about winning at any cost. There is a dangerous tribalism at work today, where partisan and group loyalties now trump any sense of the common good. These days, our approach to politics is more like rooting for different sports teams than about finding some sense of common purpose, and anyone who doesn't wear our team's jersey is the enemy.

This leads to endless division, and reaching any notion of the common good or any compromise seems increasingly impossible. Writing in *The New York Times*, Amanda Taub observed, " . . . Americans have become

---

1    Walter Brueggemann, *Hopeful Imagination: Prophetic Voices in Exile* (Minneapolis: Fortress Press, 1986), 2.

more willing to defend their party against any perceived threat, and to demand that their politicians take uncompromisingly partisan stands."[2]

Political parties are fragmenting, and each faction has their own view about what's gone wrong in the country and what should be done. New political organizations are popping up each day, funded by millionaires and billionaires, seeking to influence what issues we're paying attention to, to who runs for office, and who wins. Groups like the alt-right, Tea Party, Occupy Wall Street, and others have all sought to shape and control public discourse. Corporations and unions can operate as political battering rams. And there are a burgeoning number of special interest groups that now actively pursue their own narrow agendas. It's all a chaotic, messy, loud fight. A free-for-all, where winning for your side is the only thing that seems to count for anything.

As I mentioned in the Introduction, I worked on many political campaigns when I was a young man, the last one when I was a young aide on a US presidential race. I left party politics because of my profound frustration that campaigns had little to do with what I had learned from people like Mr. Rivers, Mr. Petker, and Mr. Brundidge. Politics failed to reflect what matters in people's lives. This obsession of winning at any cost now drives so much of politics and public life, not just campaigns and elections. It permeates all facets of governing, our public debates, and interest group maneuverings.

But winning for what, for whom? Is there some larger *common* purpose in mind? Are we working toward creating some kind of shared lives?

I was once asked in a magazine interview what my ideal notion of politics is. The interviewer was surprised when I said that the public square would be filled with competing ideas, with diverse people and groups arguing for their perspectives. The goal was not to find agreement

---

2    Amanda Taub, "Why Americans Vote 'Against Their Interest': Partisanship," *The New York Times*, April 12, 2017, https://www.nytimes.com/2017/04/12/upshot/why-americans-vote-against-their-interest-partisanship.html.

on everything, I argued, but to figure out enough of what we share in common so we can make progress together. But we are a far cry from that idea. Winning, at any cost, has taken over, holding hostage our politics and community life, damaging our collective ability to solve problems, and undermining our spirit.

## Separating at the Seams

Second, our society is separating at the seams. In *The Big Sort*, Bill Bishop writes that Americans are gathering with other like-minded people to live in particular geographic areas and communities.[3] We are sorting ourselves out by partisan views and political parties, income, and a collection of demographic factors. Bishop argues that we are no longer living together. It is a new kind of segregated life. (Though for many people of color and lower incomes, such segregation has been a fact of life for generations.)

And we are separated by much more than where we live. We concoct our very own newsfeeds and news consumption based on what conforms to our own reality. From over 400,000 podcasts, we pick and choose those that affirm, even inflame, our preexisting views.

On college campuses, there are so-called "safe spaces" created to "protect" students from having to hear differing points of view that may seem troubling or hurtful to them.

Meanwhile, faith leaders, whom we might expect—indeed hope— to bring us together and challenge us to be better, often act to divide us. Some of us now worship at places where our beliefs and convictions go unquestioned, where we are emboldened with messages that we must somehow separate ourselves from non-believers or those who believe differently than we do.

*New York Times* columnist David Brooks has often written that politics

---

3   Bill Bishop, *The Big Sort: Why the Clustering of Like-Minded America Is Tearing Us Apart* (New York: Mariner Books, 2009).

and public life are becoming driven by a defiant self-centeredness. "We probably have to scale back the culture of autonomy that was appropriate for the 1960s but that has since gone too far," he argues.[4]

Over the past three decades, I have conducted study after study about how people feel about their lives and society—including studies on materialism and consumerism, politics, health care, and education, to name a few—and I have found a growing and deepening frustration, indeed sadness, over the extent to which people are fixated on their own good.

When we keep ourselves apart from one another, it is easier to question the motives of others. It becomes easier to stereotype, create bigoted caricatures, even demonize. When we do not have shared experiences with one another, we take short cuts in our understanding of one another—short cuts that often lead us dangerously astray.

Most of us abhor tendencies to stereotype others. We find ourselves cringing when we hear people stamp others with sweeping judgment. And yet, it is happening all around us.

## More Voices—and Many Are Aggrieved

Third, more voices make up our public discourse—and many are aggrieved. Arguably, our public square is more diverse now than at any other time in our nation's history. Our public square has expanded. It is a better reflection of who we are, and this is something we should celebrate.

But how can we hear all these voices? How do we communicate with each other? How do we find shared values and any sense of common ground? Where do we even come together to do this?

And not only are there more voices, but so many of us are aggrieved as well. Each and every day, different groups in society are searching to express their grievances—to be heard, acknowledged, and addressed—from Black

---

4  David Brooks, "How to Fix Politics," *The New York Times*, April 12, 2016, https://www.nytimes.com/2016/04/12/opinion/how-to-fix-politics.html.

Lives Matter, to the LGBTQ community, to women, to Native Americans, to the white working class voter, to middle class folks who can no longer afford to send their kid to community college. Everyone seems to be aggrieved.

Donna Hicks, in her thoughtful book *Dignity*, addresses part of the challenge we face today. She argues we must pay much greater attention to people's sense of dignity. She explains, "Offering care and attention is, I now believe, at the heart of treating people with dignity."[5] Further, that the "integration of the experience of others into our worldview may sound simple, but what we must add to the task is the need to develop not just a cognitive understanding of others' points of view but also the 'feeling of what happens' to them."[6]

The more voices that make up our public discourse the harder it is to hear everyone. And hearing is not the only task. We must find ways to bridge our divides and make progress together. But how? Our task is to welcome all these different voices, find ways to make room for them, and make sense of them.

## Loss of Trust

Fourth, there is a profound loss of trust in our leaders and institutions. I recently asked a group of foundation presidents what keeps them awake at night. One said that our leaders and institutions have decayed to the point that it's extraordinarily difficult to solve any of the challenges we face as a society.

When I ask people in local communities to name leaders and organizations they trust, their lists are mighty short. Many of the leaders and institutions intended to support our lives are disconnected from what matters

---

5   Donna Hicks, *Dignity: Its Essential Role in Resolving Conflict* (New Haven, Connecticut: Yale University Press, 2013), xii.

6   Hicks, 23.

most to us. We fear they will impose unwanted and ineffective solutions on our communities—often from afar. At times, we believe these groups and leaders use our communities as their own playing fields, pursuing their own agendas and goals rather than strengthening our communities.

And not only has trust in government suffered; we have lost trust in a host of our institutions as well. Between 1973 and 2016, our confidence in public schools dropped from 58 to 30 percent, even though some of us report still liking our local schools. Confidence in banks has plummeted from 60 to 27 percent. Religious institutions of all faiths and denominations have lost relevance to many of us. Trust in Congress is at an all-time low—sinking from 42 to just 9 percent.[7]

In *The New Yorker's* "How to Restore Your Faith in Democracy," Joshua Rothman profiled the philosopher Charles Taylor. In his piece, he explains:

> *Taylor believes that, as individuals, we derive our sense of selfhood from shared values that are, in turn, embodied in public institutions. When those institutions change, those changes reverberate within us: they can seem to endanger the very meanings of our lives. It's partly for this reason that events in the political world can devastate us so intimately, striking us with the force of a breakup or a death.*[8]

And I know this loss of trust is the case because of my experience. I have spent my entire career researching and working with organizations that have been badly battered by a loss of trust and relevance. I have partnered with United Way Worldwide, which has sought to transform itself from a federated funder of local agencies to an organization seeking to

---

7   "Confidence in Institutions," Gallup, https://news.gallup.com/poll/1597/confidence-institutions. aspx.

8   Joshua Rothman, "How to Restore Your Faith in Democracy," *The New Yorker*, November 11, 2016, https://www.newyorker.com/culture/persons-of-interest/ how-to-restore-your-faith-in-democracy.

transform communities. I have guided public libraries at the local, state, and national levels in what it means to reposition themselves as a civic engine as the world around them has fundamentally altered. I have worked with numerous public school systems that people see as fortresses fighting to keep their communities at bay.

When important institutions and leaders fail to uphold a *relationship* of connection and trust with the people they serve, it is felt as a violation of a solemn promise. It rocks our sense of security and control and interdependence.

## THE HEART OF THE MATTER

In Newtown, when faced with upheaval and uncertainty, the community chose to band together. This didn't mean that people left behind their differing points of view or their competing ideas about what should happen. But amid their differences, and in the midst of their pain and suffering, they created a way to make sense of where they were and what it would take to move forward, however imperfect and unsatisfying.

As a country—as people in our communities—we find ourselves facing a host of challenges, but rather than work together, we are entangled in a free-for-all of sorts, where the direction of society is up for grabs. And people are fighting over who will author the next chapter of our shared history.

At times, it seems that we are all speaking a different language and are unable to hear one another. Our existing ideas of trust, civility, and reciprocity are no longer equipped to deal with the changing context. How did we get into this mess? Surely, it didn't just happen overnight. Nor is it simply due to the last presidential election.

Starting some 30 years ago, I began taking trips across the country every few years to interview people from all walks of life about the state of politics, their lives, and their hopes and concerns. These conversations underscore the fundamental nature of the challenge we face today—and its sheer depth. Understanding this reality can help us make sense of what's happening around us now and help us ascertain what it will take to get out of our current situation.

Let me give you a quick tour of what I have learned from these conversations. Pay close attention to the shifting nature of people's core concerns and emotions over these three decades.

- **1990: Anger.** My original report was called *Citizens and Politics: A View from Main Street America.* This was the first national study that revealed that Americans were not apathetic about politics but felt pushed out and impotent. At the time, people were turning to blunt instruments in an effort to regain control of *politics.* This included Ross Perot's run, constitutional balanced budget amendments, and term limits. People's rampant ire about politics was evident even amid the widespread sense of patriotism sweeping the country due to the nation's show of immense power in the first Gulf War.

- **1992: Felt-Unknown.** People started to express what might be called a *felt-unknown*—an inkling that something more fundamental was off in the country and their lives. But they couldn't fully articulate it or give it a name. People were no longer just angry about politics; they were worried the political system wasn't up to the task of addressing their growing concerns.

- **1995: Sadness.** People's anger and felt-unknown gave way to a fundamentally different emotion: a deep *lament* that the nation had not made progress on their nagging concerns. By now, they could more clearly define these as economic opportunity and security slipping away; unfair taxes and misguided government spending; and an emerging two class society. People began to say that individuals would need to play a much more active role in the political process to reverse current trends.

- **1998: Retreat.** People had not seen any improvement in the conditions that troubled them, so they made the following decision:

The only reasonable and rational action was to *retreat* into close-knit circles of families and friends. This step was an attempt to gain some semblance of control over their changing lives and remove themselves from the disdainful world of politics and public life. Still, there was a growing chorus that the individual must step forward to create the change people sought.

- **2003: False Hope.** The next time I went across the country, people had witnessed the vast display of patriotism that followed September 11th. This had given them a sense of renewed hope that the country and their lives could move in a better direction. But, over time, they became deeply frustrated that this show of patriotism offered nothing more than a *false start* to repairing the nation's politics and public life. Thus, people made the decision to retreat even further. They were looking for everyday heroes to help change the course of their communities and the nation.

- **2012: Bereft.** After the Great Recession, people told me that politics and the political system had become largely irrelevant to them. The currency of public discussion had entirely shifted to be on people, their lives, and their daily concerns. Americans were now bereft of a sense of possibility about their lives and the country. They yearned to get back to basics—to ignite compassion, openness and humility, and concern for the common good in daily life. The solution was to kick-start a new path—a new way forward—for the people and the country.

- **2015: Back to Basics.** I asked people what would restore their belief in our ability to get things done together with a can-do spirit. Their answer: Americans must return to being "builders"—to find a way to come together and put the country on a better path.

Of course, it would be easy to turn away from this history and focus solely on the phenomenon of Donald Trump. The argument is that if only we elect better national leaders everything will return to normal. But drawing that conclusion would be a bad mistake. The Trump election only brings to a boil long-simmering trends. We are increasingly separating from one another. A contentious tone dominates our public discourse. There's a profound sense of mistrust of our institutions and leaders. This didn't start just in 2016. More fundamental steps are required than simply changing who sits in the White House or Congress.

We are living in an environment in which a competition is taking place over people's desire to be heard. By and large, we are not communicating with each other—but past each other. The conversation is not joined up. In fact, it is grossly disjointed.

The problem is that the less we hear one another, the more the volume gets turned up. Rage emerges. And the more any notion of the truth gets put up for grabs the more people's sense of reality is undermined. When someone's reality is undermined, his or her sense of dignity is denied. Bitterness takes root. Less gets done.

We have much work to do.

## OUR WAY FORWARD

The very first time I walked into Newtown's town hall, on my right I could see Pat's office and the city council chamber where we would hold all the task force meetings. Before entering Pat's office, I found myself turning to my left.

There, I spotted two signs taped to an interior glass wall. Both signs now hang in my office. The first one read: "We are Sandy Hook. We Choose Love." The second one stated: "Our collective strength and resilience will be an example to the rest of the world."

As the person—an outsider at that—leading the task force deliberations, I was struck by the strength and resilience of the people of Newtown. Even as people expressed anger and rage and sorrow and sought to come to grips with a tragedy that shocked not just their community but the entire nation, these discussions were notable for what they lacked: acrimony, finger-pointing, and posturing. I witnessed a preponderance of openness in people. Tough, hard discussions took place, as well as deep listening.

I watched parents of Sandy Hook first-graders, business people, current and former Sandy Hook students, and others express gut-wrenching concerns about whether to return to the current school site, what it would take to deal with lasting effects of trauma on the surviving children, how they were struggling with the loss of life, and what it would take to bring about stability in the community.

Many times, I stood in the middle of the room leading these sessions in front of townspeople and a battery of media fighting back my own tears. There are few words to comfort those who experience such devastating loss. The pain never goes away. At the same time, something quite remarkable unfolded in the aftermath of Newtown's tragedy.

There, in the face of unimaginable circumstances, when so many parts of the process and so many people could have splintered apart, the community worked to hold itself together.

Now, amid the noise and confusion enveloping the nation, it's our turn to build our strength and resilience. We must rediscover what we share in common and how we can build upon it.

Part II:

# SHARED
# RESPONSIBILITY

# TURN OUTWARD

When my daughter Emily was 21, she and I went to Germany to visit the Nazi death camp Dachau. I needed to stare fear and despair in the face and to know my faith more intimately.

Upon returning to Munich for dinner that night after our visit, Emily could see how unsettled I was. The camp was still calling my name. I had something more to find there. I was being pulled back to the scene of the inexplicable. Emily then granted me the greatest gift she could have ever given me—permission to go find what was missing within me. Looking up from her dinner plate, in her small quiet voice, she firmly instructed me to go back to Dachau the next day.

"Go," she said. "Take as much time as you need."

That night, I slept in fits and starts. I rose at dawn and caught the earliest train back to Dachau. I arrived at the camp before seven o'clock in the morning. It was closed. I sat alone on a stone wall bordering the camp, in trepidation of what I would experience that day. I wrote in my journal, struggling with my fears.

Then, all of a sudden, something moved me. I stood up and walked down the long path toward the main gate. The gate that infamously reads: "Work will set you free." It was closed, but for some reason, I went up to it, put my hands on it, and gently pushed.

The gate opened. I walked in.

No living person was there. There were only the souls of those who had perished. I could feel their presence. I made my way to the courtyard, where prisoners had been forced to line up each morning and be counted. Each evening they'd repeat the scene, the numbers dwindling from one lineup to the next.

The courtyard, all dirt, seemed vast. I remember it to be the size of a football field or two. I slowly made my way to the middle of it. There, alone, I stood for over an hour. I remained absolutely still. I felt I had come face-to-face with evil. At one point, I shut my eyes and began to chant Hebrew prayers I've known since childhood. I suppose it was my way to make my voice heard. It was my way not to succumb to fear. This was a form of action—declaring what I am *for*, in a place that stands for everything humanity is against. Tears rolled down my face.

The Jewish tradition teaches that if you save one person, you save the world. This simple lesson is an entreaty to step forward. It is a plea to make ourselves visible, to take small steps to create a better society.

I routinely remind myself of this teaching and ask myself how well I'm fulfilling it. In doing so, my main task is not merely to land the next big project, get more media attention, or give yet another speech, but also to make sure that what I do holds purpose and meaning. Implementing my work is never enough. The test is if the work mattered in someone's life.

Of course, I can always find ways to run faster and harder. I want my work to have the greatest and widest reach possible. But the real question is will I slow down long enough to hear the answer to this question, and then will I heed the response? As I stood alone in the middle of the Dachau courtyard, the world stopped, and I understood that success is not about achieving what you desire. It is doing something that calls us to improve our shared humanity. But to focus on our shared humanity, we must have people in our line of sight.

Turning outward is about the call to fulfill the deepest yearning within you to improve the lives of others and to bring greater purpose and meaning to your own life. To be turned outward is to make your community the reference point for all you do. To know that there is something larger that must inform and drive, even supersede, whatever programs, processes, initiatives, and data that consume our attention.

This is Principle 1: Turn outward.

## A MINDSET

Fundamentally, turning outward is a mindset—a stance, a posture, an orientation. You can't buy it. It's not a technical skill you possess, nor is it something you just learn about. It is the direction you choose to face in doing the work you do as you live your life.

Only by turning outward can you locate the community before you—whether it's a geographic area, a community of worship, or a community of interest. Only then can you truly make your way into it. Only then can you see and hear others in that community. It's when we're turned outward that we can really see what's around us—the good, bad, and ugly.

In *Upstream*, Mary Oliver speaks to the notion of being turned outward when she writes that it is "necessary to be rooted, again, in the world."[1] Yes, we must be rooted in our communities and the world around us in order to discover the potential of what we share, the possibilities for building together, and the opportunities to make progress together.

Because of the noise and confusion that surrounds us, we all make wrong turns along the way, and each of these turns can seem as right and as good as the one before it. But after a while, you can feel as if you are spinning in circles. I am asking you to squarely plant your feet. Now, turn yourself outward toward others and your community. Open your eyes and heart. Let the world come in.

---

1   Mary Oliver, *Upstream: Selected Essays* (London: Penguin, 2016), 100.

## WHY TURN OUTWARD

For me, turning outward is first and foremost about people. When all is said and done, we all wish to improve others' lives through what we do. Isn't this what you care most about? Why you spend so much time working against such great odds? Isn't your hope to make your community and our society stronger, more decent, more whole?

To be focused on people is to know what matters to them—the aspirations they hold for their lives and communities. It is to know what actions will truly make a difference to people. Context matters. Doing things that are *necessary*, not simply *nice* to do, matters.

Only when we turn outward is human dignity possible. Think about it. How else could it happen? Only when I am able to keep people in my line of sight am I able to stay true to my own sense of purpose. Then I can lean in to my own life with meaning and connection.

Turning outward is also about the impact you want to achieve. The efforts you pursue are about *improving* people's lives. When you are particularly effective, maybe a bit lucky, people's lives can be *transformed*.

Without the possibility of such progress, why step forward and work so hard? Is it simply to get ahead? So you can write yet one more memo? Raise yet more money? Gather up more volunteers? Gain more status and power? Toward what end, I ask you, do you try so much? These aren't rhetorical questions for me; I actually want to make a real, tangible difference in people's lives.

## NOT INWARD, BUT OUTWARD

I find that when we need to turn outward the most, we often turn inward. Many times, we don't even recognize that we've turned inward or that the organizations and initiatives we work with have turned inward. But it's happened.

Inwardness is an incessant focus on our own internal processes, problem solving, programs, and perspectives. It's not that these things are intrinsically bad; in fact, they're all necessary. The problem is when we turn inward at the expense of the people and communities we seek to improve. The more pressure we're under—the more we want our efforts to be relevant for people in communities, the more we seek to generate positive impact in people's lives, the more we attempt to marshal our collective resources—the more inward we turn. We come up with yet another strategic plan, reorganize the boxes in our organizational charts, and rename program areas. But if we are not turned outward and in tune with what matters most to people, how will we know if these are the steps that will make us more effective?

I see inwardness take hold when we become overly reliant on using data. We must remember that data can tell us only so much about people's experiences. I remember working in the Asylum Hill neighborhood of Hartford, Connecticut, when all the data stated that the big problems were education and jobs. Many institutions wanted to double down on initiatives in these areas. But when we engaged residents there, they told us they wanted a safer, more connected community. It's not that the data wasn't vital or true; it's that it missed what actually mattered and needed attention in these people's lives.

The same thing happens when we confuse marketing for genuine listening. While attending a conference on community change, a group leader tried to placate my questions about authentically engaging residents of communities by saying, "Don't worry, we have a good marketing plan!" Her idea of engagement was to *sell* her pre-set plan to the community. She was looking inward rather than outward.

Inwardness takes on other forms, too. For instance, we live in a world in which generating long lists of activities consumes our daily lives, as if busyness equals purpose and impact. We become enamored with our own initiatives and programs and keep our heads down, all the while blindly insisting our efforts truly matter to people. We ramp up the volume of our declarations to get people's attention, as if people will find a sense of possibility and hope in that.

No one sets out to be inward. It just happens—to all of us. It's human nature. We don't realize that an inwardness seeps into what we do. Even into who we have become. It's how we're trained. What we're told to do. What conferences promote. Like a virus, inwardness spreads if left unchecked.

But inwardness won't help us effectively see and hear people. People won't gain more control over their lives. A genuine sense of possibility and hope won't take hold. Nor will people feel a part of something larger than themselves.

I see inwardness in the incessant push to use best practices and scale initiatives. Under the right conditions, both strategies have their rightful time and place. But too often we lose a critical part of the story: "why" and "how" something worked in one community or another. Community context is lost in our urgent quest to implement a chosen answer. This one-size-fits-all approach doesn't account for the reality of people's lives and the varying conditions of different communities.

## LOST IN THE MECHANICS

When I led a discussion in Battle Creek, Michigan, local leaders repeatedly described their community as being jaded and frustrated. Endless turf battles had led to the crippling of community efforts. There weren't enough trusted leaders and organizations to rally the community and address local challenges.

The community said it was tired of initiatives and programs that started one day only to fade away. This undermined people's confidence that anything could get done. In fact, the prevailing way of doing business in town was to do things *to* people rather than *with* people.

A few years after holding the Battle Creek discussion, I began working with a group that was launching a big community-wide initiative that promised big change. I remember feeling bewildered when the group showed me pages upon pages of dense academic articles explaining their new approach. I simply couldn't understand them. They brought out complex charts that illustrated how this effort would work. But these charts seemed to require an engineering degree to make sense of them. They listed all the committees and subcommittees to coordinate their every activity. As if managing all that were even possible. To me, they had created a new social Erector Set to impose upon the community and the people who lived there.

Despite good intentions, we regularly devise solutions that are so complex, so damn complicated, so incredibly focused on the intricacies of process, that we lose sight of the people we are trying to help. I've seen this happen with efforts in small towns seeking to bring people together; in religious congregations that are trying to find ways for congregants to put their faith into action; in multibillion-dollar organizations intent on securing more change.

Our approaches can become mechanical, and managing them becomes our main focus. Select groups of professionals drive discussions, decisions, and actions. Meanwhile, everyday people and other groups in communities—all with time, energy, and resources to offer—get pushed aside, or left out. Somehow, we think that devising complex, comprehensive solutions is the answer to our challenges. Maybe we think they give us more credibility or that we appear to be more professional and expert in our ways. Perhaps they make us feel more worthy and important.

Many of the problems we face do demand complex responses. But amid these demands, we must work diligently to maintain a posture of being turned outward. This takes constantly reminding ourselves of our purpose in acting—what we are actually trying to achieve—and what it takes to make a real difference. Otherwise, all our best-laid plans may sound good to us and to others, but fail to either help people or create the impact they need.

## ONLY YOU CAN DO THIS

With each passing day, the choice of whether you turn outward becomes ever more critical. Noise and confusion are disorienting for all of us. It dispirits us. At the same time, inwardness only takes us farther away from the people we long to serve and the impact we want to achieve. Current times beg us to engage in a fundamentally different way.

But, what if we don't? Will you or I be satisfied if so many people feel they've lost their sense of dignity? Will we be okay if there are those who believe they no longer have a voice or are seen and heard? If people lose even more faith in the institutions and organizations needed to get things done? When mistrust prevails? Maybe we should simply allow these conditions to persist? Throw up our hands in frustration and disgust? Succumb?

I know you will not succumb. Nor will I.

Still, I also know fear can set in when trying to turn outward. Fear is always present in making this kind of turn. Being fearless in our lives, in how we engage with others and the world around us, is impossible. Fear is always present amid our deepest desires. Moses felt it at the burning bush. I felt it sitting in a hospital bed and when the three men came into my life and challenged me to get up and get going. We feel it when we try to alter our daily routines. None of us can outrun fear. You must know that it is there, especially when you decide to make a turn. It is only natural.

But here's what I also know: You gain purpose and strength when you turn outward. When you are focused on our shared lives and what we can build together.

In some respects I am asking you not just to turn outward toward the community. I am asking you to *re*-turn to something you already know like the back of your hand—the most basic, decent, and hopeful parts that exist within you. Call on these parts. They want to hear from you.

Stop long enough in your busy life to push open the gates to the world around you. Then turn yourself outward. Open yourself up. Let the world in.

# Principle 2

# DISCOVER WHAT
# WE SHARE

Ralph Ellison, the great American author, a huge favorite of mine, was also an aspiring musician. In the introduction to *Flying Home*, Ellison's collection of short stories, John F. Callahan recounts a time when Ellison received criticism after one of his early trumpet recitals:

> *More soothing and salutary was the scolding administered in private by Hazel Harrison, the concert pianist and confidante . . . Harrison's honesty gave Ellison the key to the relationship between the artist and his audience—"you must always play your best, even if it's only in the waiting room at Chehaw Station, because in this country there'll always be a little man hidden behind the stove" and "he'll know the music, and the tradition, and the standards of musicianship required for whatever you set out to perform." Harrison's words made a deep impression on Ellison. Embracing a very stern discipline, he resolved to perform or write always as if the little man at Chehaw Station were looking over his shoulder.*[1]

---

1   Ralph Ellison, *Flying Home: And Other Stories* (New York: Vintage, 1998), xv–xvi.

Ellison's experience speaks to the nature of being purposeful; the need to always apply oneself; to be supremely conscious, ever aware, of what one is doing and why. His experience reminds us of a voice we can hear inside ourselves when it comes to our own engagement in the world: *What is our purpose in acting?*

It is so damn hard to hear this voice nowadays. It is drowned out by the noise and cynicism that overwhelms so much of our lives. We are isolated from one another, split off by the tribalism that can divide us. This voice becomes extinguished by feeling the need to win at all costs.

We crowd out the necessary room for our meaningful and authentic engagement when we embrace inward solutions. These solutions undercut people's ability to be seen and heard when being seen and heard is what we all long for. They undermine people's desire to be part of a common effort to tackle our shared challenges. They take us further away from the very people and communities we seek to serve and support. They are a mechanical approach when we need a distinctly human response.

In her book *When I Was a Child I Read Books*, Marilynne Robinson speaks to the danger of believing mechanical approaches are the answer to our most basic long-term problems. She rightly warns us: "Our problem with ourselves, which is much larger and vastly older than science, has by no means gone into abeyance since we learned to make penicillin or to split the atom." Robinson wants us to engage "in the more general project of human self-awareness and self-assertion."[2] This engagement is what makes us alive—human.

But in our daily lives, purposefulness is overtaken by daily pressures. What does the boss or a colleague think? What does the budget say? How much time do I have to complete this task? How can I choose solutions to problems where I am not at risk? What will other people say about me? What's my status and power? Daily rhythms—some from work, others

---

2   Marilynne Robinson, *When I Was a Child I Read Books: Essays* (New York: Farrar, Straus, and Giroux, 2012), 16.

from our home lives, and still others generated elsewhere—create molds and ruts that shape how we engage.

The purposefulness that Ellison came to think about can silently, even unknowingly, get pushed aside amid all the racket and confusion that make up our current times. It eludes us. But it needn't.

It's vital to recognize just how often we embrace assumptions about how things work and how these assumptions can take on a kind of default mode in our individual and collective minds. We believe things will always be a certain way, and they won't or can't ever change. And so we come to assume that we live in a world in which we are all destined to be divided, hyper-focused on individualism, and often at war with one another. Negativity abounds.

But these assumptions dampen, even block, our imagination to move in a new direction—a more positive direction. Sadly, we can find ourselves resigned to how things are and how we assume they will always be.

As Robinson tells us, "When we accept dismissive judgments of our community we stop having generous hopes for it."[3] Then we're stuck. Our imagination goes on hold.

Our task is to turn outward and re-instill our generous hopes, find what we share in common, and learn to build upon it productively. When we do this, we can bring a greater sense of purpose and meaning to our lives.

This is Principle 2: Discover what we share.

## THE THINGS WE SHARE

More than mere rhetoric is required to make this shift. We must actively embrace a different view of what we are seeking to create together—and what that will take. It demands that we focus on what matters to us— rather than just what I or my group cares about; what enlivens us—in

---

3  Robinson, 30.

place of what diminishes our spirit; what calls us to engage in our shared lives—instead of us separating from one another; what enables us to marshal our collective resources in our communities—versus going it alone.

Rachel Yehuda, a professor of psychiatry and neuroscience at Mount Sinai Hospital in New York City, has said, "If you want to make a society work, then you don't keep underscoring the places where you're different—you underscore your shared humanity."[4]

In our society today, we are obsessed with our differences, winning for our own side, and protecting our own turf. This assures that we will be fragmented and divided, with too many of us feeling that we are on our own. But we cannot—we will not—build cohesive, strong, and vibrant communities on this path. It's simply not possible.

Do not take my pleas for coming together as a guise for denying or diminishing our individualism and identities, our unique cultures and heritages, or our different beliefs. Nor do I aim to gloss over our differences so that we may all get along. We shouldn't pretend that we are all the same. Liking each other is not the goal either. Real differences exist among us.

But given these realities, or especially because of them, we must dedicate ourselves to honoring our differences and then finding those things we do share. This idea of what we share—isn't this the meaning of *E pluribus unum*? Out of many, one. Our nation was founded on the very idea of pluralism. But pluralism alone is not enough. Left unbridled, it is too easy for us to remain splintered.

Time and again, throughout our history, we have realized that we must come together across our differences to work on what we share, address ugly stains on our nation's fabric, make progress, and strive for a more perfect union. We have done this on big issues from the founding of the country to the abolition of slavery to child welfare laws; to issues focused on our own community or neighborhood such as neighborhood safety, public schools, and regenerating our local economy.

---

4   Sebastian Junger, *Tribe: On Homecoming and Belonging* (New York: Twelve, 2016), 127.

There are times we forget this critical lesson of discovering our shared concerns and taking shared action. It's as if amnesia sets in. We must remember that our task is to not wallow in our differences and especially not to inflame simply out of a desire to win an argument.

## FEARING THE OTHER

There is a huge difference between a disposition that seeks to divide and take up sides and that sees those different from ourselves as "the other," and one that is out to inspire, transcend, and build.

In the Bible there is the story of when Joshua takes over leadership from Moses and encounters someone standing before him, sword in hand. It's an angel. But before Joshua recognizes the angel, he defiantly asks, "Are you one of us or one of our enemies?"

David Wolpe, in his book *In Speech and in Silence*, suggests that the angel's response of "No," as opposed to "Neither one," implies that "Joshua has been thinking the wrong way, that his whole framing of the question cannot serve."[5] Poor Joshua had become entrenched in a disposition of division and negativity.

Listen to our public debates, the media, our daily conversations—so much of it reflects this zero-sum language, a language that undermines our confidence in one another, that makes us fear the other, that tells us to win at any cost. A disposition of division and negativity closes off possibilities for us to create positive and productive progress. Instead, we must focus on what we seek to build together, and not what we are working to tear down.

## FOCUS ON SHARED ASPIRATIONS

I find that when people come together with others and focus on their shared aspirations for their lives and community, the type of fundamental

---

5   David J. Wolpe, *In Speech and in Silence: The Jewish Quest for God* (New York: Henry Holt and Company, 1992), 61–62.

shift I'm calling for occurs. People express what they are for rather than what they're against.

Focusing on shared aspirations is very different from focusing on our problems, which often leads people to reel off a laundry list of complaints. When this happens, people want to know why these problems haven't already been solved, who is responsible for fixing them, and who they can blame for not solving them. It leads us to lay the culpability solely on others, with little to no responsibility for helping make improvements ourselves. We must not come from a place of complaining.

Focusing on shared aspirations is also very different from laying out a pie-in-the-sky vision for our communities. Such visions are often rooted in people's dreams about the future, offering utopian views about what society should be. But such utopian ideas are unattainable. Have you ever wondered why so many efforts at creating such visions fizzle out? They lack relevance to people's daily challenges. They provide little sense of genuine possibility. They're not connected to our daily realities and what matters most to us in our day-to-day lives.

Ask anyone about their aspirations for their lives and communities and they will tell you about things that truly matter to them. Try this yourself. Around your dinner table, at work, at your place of worship, in your neighborhood, ask people: What are your aspirations for your community? Listen carefully to their responses. What are the qualities of their aspirations?

Our aspirations come from our gut. They project onto things that we seek, that are actionable, doable, and achievable. I've seen this happen in hundreds of communities over the past 30 years. When goals and plans are rooted in the aspirations of the people in the community, they are more. I can still remember working in Greenville, South Carolina, where people from across the community had come together to talk about their local public schools.

They were part of a multiyear initiative to reconnect communities and schools that we had created at the invitation of then-State Superintendent of Schools Barbara Nielsen. I always believed that Barbara was a brave and innovative soul to have thought up and spearheaded this effort. Over time, the initiative would spread to communities across South Carolina and then on to Mobile, Alabama, and then to communities throughout Alabama, Ohio, and elsewhere in the nation.

When the Greenville effort first began, most leaders there warned me that it was a fool's errand. At the time, the community was deeply divided between and among African Americans and whites, old-timers and new-comers (best symbolized by the new BMW plant in town), and wealthier and poorer residents.

The leaders said that people would never show up, let alone sit in the same room with one another, and, if they did, they certainly wouldn't be able to talk about an issue that had for generations sat at the center of the community's strife.

But people did come, and they returned repeatedly. Over many months, growing numbers of Greenville residents committed and recommitted themselves to a conversation that ultimately produced a public covenant on the relationship between their schools and community.

These conversations began with a single question, "What are your aspirations for the community?" Just starting with that simple question enabled people who had been disagreeing for years to have a different conversation, and they were able to see that the kind of community they wanted to live in was something they shared. They all wanted to find a way forward. This didn't happen all at once, but eventually emerged through fits and starts.

At the heart of their aspirations was a set of three interconnected values. There was the desire for the community finally to step up and hold public schools accountable for their actions, which is something people said they had failed to do for years. There was the commitment among residents to finally say they must provide sufficient and equitable resources for schools to succeed. And there was the belief that parents and the community at large must finally take full responsibility for being supportive of the schools and being actively involved in the lives of all children.

For far too long, these Greenville residents pointed out, the community, schools, and at times the local government, sat comfortably at arms'
length from the most important business they had to do: educate and
raise their community's children. In these conversations, their shared aspirations called for not only the public schools to take action but also for
parents, neighbors, business, nonprofits, and others in the community to
take action as well. The public schools and rearing good kids were to be a
community undertaking. By focusing on their shared aspirations, people
who might otherwise never share a room or a meal shared their deepest
hopes for the community.

Years later, we called to check in with some of the individuals
involved in the Greenville effort. I especially remember one older African-American woman who had lived in the community for many years
and had initially been skeptical about the initiative. Upon reflection, she
said that simply being in the same room with the others was worth every
minute of her time.

She, like others, was moved by the fact that such a diverse and disparate group had come to know their aspirations for the community—and
that such aspirations still existed within themselves. A sense of faith was
restored in people because they were able to figure out what they shared in
common after so many painful years of endless arguments, finger point-
ing, and an ingrained belief that change was not possible.

As I mentioned previously, in *Hopeful Imagination*, Walter Brueggemann writes that in order to move on to something new, you must first
have knowledge about where you are. Surely, his insight has much to do
with the need to see and know reality for what it is. But his words are also
about much more than that.

What propels people and communities forward is when they know
their aspirations and where they want to go. I am not speaking here about
identifying a specific policy or program; in fact, the rush to such specifics
is what often mires people and communities in stilted conversations that
lead to divisive solution wars.

Instead, there is something we must know before we even entertain such solutions, something that is more telling and revealing, and something that ultimately is more durable. We must know what is it that we seek to co-create in our lives and community. It is by people discovering and articulating their aspirations that they can set the very trajectory on which they seek to move ahead.

When I hear people talk about their shared aspirations in spite of their differences—in their views, the color of their skin, religious beliefs, income, and geography—there is a profound ability to recognize what we share. This is what happened in Greenville; it's what I see happen in communities every day.

Once we see our shared aspirations, something else wonderful occurs. People say that no one leader, no one organization, no one initiative—however well endowed, designed, or orchestrated—could ever achieve these shared aspirations on its own. We need each other.

As human beings, we are not whole without others. We often don't know what we think before we hear others speak. Connection requires others. To be engaged, you need others. Building takes one another.

Parker Palmer writes eloquently about this basic human desire in many of his books, including *Let Your Life Speak* " . . . the life that I am living is not the same as the life that wants to live in me."[6] Each of us has aspirations that we want to fulfill. We are seeking to create a better life. We want our lives to hold greater purpose and meaning. And there is no other way to do that than together.

## A NEW COVENANT

We are by definition then—whether we like it or not, whether we like one another or not—in relationship with one another. There is no way around

---

6  Parker J. Palmer, *Let Your Life Speak: Listening for the Voice of Vocation* (San Francisco, California: Jossey-Bass, 1999), 2.

it. And while this reality is as old as humankind, it is one to which we must recommit ourselves if we are to create shared lives.

But unfortunately so many of our relationships are in tatters, riddled by division and fear, undermined by narrow self-interest. Throwing up our hands in disgust about where we find ourselves will do no good. Such expressions of exasperation may give us a moment of respite, allowing us to let loose our frustrations, but this is not a productive path. To move forward, we must purposefully forge new and stronger relationships.

And so at the heart of discovering what we share sits a covenant—a civic covenant—with one another. A civic covenant is about how we choose to engage with one another, take mutual responsibility for producing a better society, and step forward to do the work that needs to be done, together.

An individual leader cannot declare this covenant. No special commission appointed by the US president or housed at some prestigious university can produce a new report about what it will be. There is no decree. It can only emerge over time through our interactions. In Greenville, people produced such a covenant focused on the relationship between schools and the community. Many communities I have worked with have created such covenants.

But mostly what I have in mind here concerns something even more fundamental: how we even see each other, how we approach one another, how we imagine and act on common challenges and move forward together. In our legalistic and litigious society, contracts abound and rules circumscribe our actions. Now, we must pursue something more profoundly human.

Think of our civic covenant as a living arrangement, created and recreated each and every day, through the combination of the various actions we each take. Friends have such implicit agreements. Families have them too. Religious faiths have them. They all come about through a commitment to purposefulness.

## THE NEED FOR AUTHENTIC HOPE

We cannot build shared lives and common action on a foundation of false hope. And so greater purposefulness also calls us to reject false hope.

Yet so often false hope riddles our shared lives. Typically it's inadvertent; other times, more suspect. We promise to transform a community's public schools in two years when we know it will take much longer. We declare we'll end poverty through a new complex initiative that bears little relationship to the challenge and people's lived experiences. We proclaim that with enough funding we'll solve the opioid crisis, when we know it takes more than just money. We say we will change the culture of our organization through some new half-baked effort. Surely, you can add in your own examples.

Pronouncements about "fixing" societal problems—as if we are fixing a car or plugging a leak in our roof—only add to people's sense of frustration and cynicism. Many problems are not amenable to quick fixes. And when we insist on pursuing such a path, we create false hope.

False hope is deepened when we say we want to engage the community in addressing shared problems, but then take an inward course. It spreads when expectations for change fail to reflect reality, such as when we believe that's the best route to attract supporters, funders, or attention, which doesn't actually accomplish anything. People feel they are being sold yet another bill of goods. Attempts to influence their emotions and the truth leave them feeling manipulated.

Why do we go down this tired, worn-out path? Maybe we assume that if we focus on our real challenges and our true losses, we'll undermine or destroy hope. Maybe we believe that to acknowledge fear and despair contaminates hope. But nothing could be further from the truth. The seeds of hope are to be found in the very messiness and pain—and yes, the goodness and joy—inherent in our daily lives. I know this firsthand.

It's time to take a different path: authentic hope. Authentic hope grows when people come together across dividing lines and can see and hear one another. When tough issues are put on the table for public discussion—not because anyone expects them to be solved overnight, but because by acknowledging them we recognize people's reality and offer a sense of possibility that some change can occur. Authentic hope can be seen when we set out on a course for change and take small steps forward that demonstrate progress.

Authentic hope spreads when we tell stories of people striving to improve their conditions, especially when those stories contain their struggles and even failures. Then they're real.

None of this is about a utopian vision. It's about people's lives, their aspirations, and the relationships we have. In one way or another, nearly every point I make in this book deals with some fundamental choice we have about the kind of hope we will create.

## SEE YOURSELF AS A CREATOR

If the goal is to discover what we share, build upon that together, and engender authentic hope, then the only way to do this is to come from a place of understanding and create a path based on that understanding. It is in the very process of creating this path that we produce meaning and connection and possibility. Indeed, we share what we produce together. We care most about those things we create.

Thus, I am calling upon all of us to see ourselves as creators. We must recognize that we hold the power and the potential to shape the world we want. We are not powerless. We are not bereft of choices. Being passive bystanders is not an option.

At the heart of the shift I am aiming for stands the belief in the inherent goodness of people. Amid the isolation, division, and evil that exists, we must remember this goodness. Over and over and over again, we must remind ourselves of this goodness.

Walt Whitman captures this notion best: "I am larger, better than I thought/I did not know I held such goodness."[7] It is our human potential

---

7    Walt Whitman, *Walt Whitman: Poetry and Prose* (New York: Library of America, 1982), 300.

that we must know and embrace and activate. The story of Moses at the burning bush tells us this. "Here I am," he declared! Never in his wildest dreams could he have predicted what he would be called to do. Nor what he would accomplish.

None of us can change the world on our own. No one is asking you or me to do that. But we each can do our part. We must release ourselves from the burden of believing we must fix everything—and all at once. Instead, we must ask: What is our contribution?

Our contributions are likely to happen in small ways. Dorothy Day tells us to take small steps—and each step will create ripples in all directions.

One of the things I love about pragmatic idealism, a branch of American philosophy, is that it calls upon us to continually take such steps forward despite the challenges before us. John Kaag writes in *American Philosophy* that pragmatic idealism "has a perfectionist streak, but its idealism is in the process, always on the way."[8] No matter how small, our efforts matter.

Through them, we can and do create a difference.

Within each of us is a restlessness and relentlessness to strive for our ideals, even though we know that we might never fully attain them. We go forth, anyway. Always.

This American tradition to live in meaningful communities with shared lives and not live alone beckons to us. I am asking you to be purposeful in being creators of a common enterprise called community. To do this, we must embrace different practices when it comes to making change, we must realize what we're capable of, and act to make our aspirations a reality.

---

8   John Kaag, *American Philosophy: A Love Story* (New York: Farrar, Straus, and Giroux, 2016), 94.

# Principle 3

# VALUE THE HUMAN SPARK

Recently, my wife Jackie and I were sitting on the town square of a small community outside Atlanta, talking about Sebastian Junger's recently published book, *Tribe: On Homecoming and Belonging*. Junger's writing is enthralling. Through a variety of stories and research, he speaks to the human desire to create and advance shared norms and ideals through common action. He talks about how people in one community after another have come together after natural disasters; how Londoners spontaneously banded together in response to the Nazi Blitz during World War II; how various tribes, centuries ago, organized themselves to ensure and protect the common good of their communities.

Despite highlighting such human triumphs, Junger tells us that he is less optimistic about where we are today. He worries not about our innate desires and capabilities—they're still intact—but about larger conditions in society that are actively crowding out people's ability to act.

In *Tribe* he writes: "[T]he beauty and the tragedy of the modern world is that it eliminates many situations that require people to demonstrate a commitment to the collective good."[1] For Junger, there is a tension between our natural desires for connection and community and the current environment in which we live.

I explained to Jackie that this concern was something I've wrestled with in one form or another throughout my 30-year career. How do we bring ourselves into the world, relate to one another, and lean into our individual lives? How do we create shared lives? I told my wife I wanted to commit the rest of my career to addressing this challenge, particularly as it relates to the value we place on people's innate capabilities to create the communities and society we want.

This certainly wasn't a new thought for me. Since the time of my childhood illness, and then my experiences with Mr. Rivers, Mr. Petker, and Mr. Brundidge, this commitment has been my single-minded pursuit. Through the actions of these three incredible men, I learned at an early age about the power of people's innate capabilities. How they help us not succumb to frustration and fear, how they propel us forward, how they give us hope.

Each of us has the inherent ability to do things, make things happen, produce things—the capacity to imagine something better than what already exists. This is what makes us human.

Religious beliefs, mythology, fables, and literature all make references to a natural spark within each of us waiting to be activated. Today, we must realize that spark exists in all of us. We must value it and make room for it, if we are to reimagine and act on the opportunity I see before us.

This is Principle 3: Value the human spark.

## STEPPING OVER THE THRESHOLD

Years ago, when I was working in Flint, Michigan, the community had descended into turmoil. Thousands upon thousands of autoworkers were

---

1   Sebastian Junger, *Tribe: On Homecoming and Belonging* (New York: Twelve, 2016), 59.

laid off in a matter of years. Shock waves shook the community. Public schools were failing. Racial tensions riddled relationships of all sorts. The people of Flint trusted few leaders and organizations to make things right.

People's livelihoods were shattered, social networks tattered, and the fabric of the larger community ripped apart. Amid the mistrust and sense of isolation, Flint residents told us they were afraid to talk with one another. And this was all long before the more recent Flint River water crisis that led to the tragic poisoning of so many children and adults there, providing yet another setback to this fiercely resilient and proud community.

At the time of my work in Flint, many of us were flummoxed by the sheer magnitude of the challenges facing the community. Lots of ideas were put on the table. Some were exactly what the community didn't need. For instance, before I got to Flint, a cadre of outside consultants developed utopian visions of what the community could become. The good folks of Flint weren't in search of utopia. They wanted decent-paying jobs, good education for their kids, and safe streets.

A more grounded idea emerged from our conversations with residents: an effort called Take-A-Step. The goal was simple enough. Find a way for people to begin to rebuild trust and see each other's innate capabilities. From there, this could form the foundation for future actions.

This was a human response to a complex set of circumstances that beset Flint. We had no illusions that it would "fix" the community. Just the opposite. It was an initial small step—and a critical one.

Imagine in your mind the narrow metal strip beneath the front door of your home. It's called a threshold. In Flint, the first-order challenge was to find a way for people to step over that threshold from their private lives into their shared community life.

We knew what wouldn't work: drumming up more noise and confusion. Like imploring people to come out from their homes and listen to more promises and false hope—they were already tired of being talked at, yelled at, and lectured. We knew that trying to strike fear in people that if they didn't engage their world would fall apart wouldn't work. Their world was already falling apart. We also rejected the idea of mobilizing people around their anger to storm city hall; we sought to create community, not one-time political wins. Actions like these might only make people retreat more deeply into their homes, further inflaming the situation.

Instead, an opportunity needed to be created for people to express what *they* were *for*—and to be a part of creating it. This is the approach we took, which allowed people in Flint to step across their thresholds. This led us to craft four questions that people could use to jump-start a safe conversation with their neighbors, friends, and others in the community:

1. What kind of community do you want to live in?
2. Why is this important to you?
3. How is that different from how you see things now?
4. What are some of the things that need to happen to create that kind of change?

We distributed these questions far and wide—to people's homes, on restaurant place mats, and through the media. We worked hand-in-hand with a diverse group of local residents such as Lee Bell at the Neighborhood Roundtable, Pete Hutchison at the Neighborhood Violence Prevention Collaborative, Vicky Hurley at Eastside Neighbors, and Lucille James at Salem Housing Task Force. They and others then encouraged people to use the questions and build new civic efforts based on them. Sure enough, it worked.

People started talking on their front porches and in laundromats. Some came together to take action. Salem Housing, a local sweat-equity housing group—a kind of local version of Habitat for Humanity—had new homeowners use the questions to think about how they wanted to become part of their neighborhoods. Local churches engaged their congregants in how to put their faith into action. The public library distributed the questions to people coming into the library, and brought people together to forge new relationships. It worked. Through these questions, people began to see the spark in one another, and it brought them together.

When I would tell people outside of Flint that I was working there, they'd look puzzled, asking "why?" They'd wonder, "Why not just let the town die? Why don't long-term residents just get up and leave?" I always responded in the same way: Who are we to tell a community to die? Besides, some people who wanted to leave couldn't afford the cost of moving. And they had no job to go to.

But there are even more important reasons. People wanted their community to live. They wanted shared lives. Flint's their *home*. A human spark resided there.

## A SPARK IN BELLAMBI

When people step over the threshold, they can create—or recreate—their shared aspirations and lives. I saw this in Australia. During a recent visit, I was updated on what was happening in Bellambi, a community in the Illawarra region, just south of Sydney. For a number of years now, Brian Smith, one of our Australian team members, has been working in Bellambi with residents, government agencies, local university staff, and nonprofits, among others.

Over the years, Bellambi has suffered from high levels of unemployment, poverty, and crime. Few amenities exist. Because of these worsening conditions, a state agency decided to conduct an evaluation of the area. It called for coordinating a laundry list of initiatives that various government agencies would "bring to the community."

But instead of rushing to implement the study's recommendations, the ad hoc group that Brian had begun to work with, which now included representatives of the state agency that sponsored the initial study, paused. As they discussed the situation, they thought better of just forging ahead. They wanted to first engage the community.

Numerous community conversations were held. At one point, 150 people were trained in using questions much like the ones used in Flint. They went to the streets of Bellambi and talked with over 1,000 people in a single day. Once the community's voice began to take shape, the group set up an open meeting to report back on what was being learned.

Jean, a long-time Bellambi resident, had seen a host of previous community-based efforts come and go. She was angry that yet another was now taking place. She decided to attend the meeting to complain about one more outside effort imposed upon her struggling community.

But Jean was startled as she listened to the insights from the community's conversations. Her genuine concerns were actually being reflected. With tears in her eyes, she stood up to say, "I came here today to tell you all this, but you already know it." Many others at the meeting felt exactly the same way Jean did. A positive buzz of energy and possibility filled the room.

On that day, a community that for years had felt descended upon, even manipulated by government agencies, outside consultants, and other groups, had begun to reimagine its opportunity, and hope for the future began to emerge among community residents.

A collection of new ideas emerged from the open meeting for how people could re-assert control over their lives. Many of them are being implemented. A rubbish and graffiti-removal initiative started almost immediately. Police acted on some of the safety concerns the community identified, including shutting down a number of long-standing drug houses. The local neighborhood center, after being moribund for years, was revitalized by community members.

Short of one year later, the community came together to celebrate its progress. Over 300 people showed up. Businesses and entrepreneurs were stepping forward in the community to identify new enterprises that could be established to increase local amenities and provide work and training opportunities. The government agencies and other groups began to rethink their plans. They could see the community had many more innate capabilities than ever imagined, and tapping those capabilities was the best place for the community to start its new journey.

Jean found a way to step over her own threshold. She was no longer sitting alone in her home frustrated, angry, and mistrustful. She had joined with others. And others from the community began to find a way to tap into their own innate capabilities to take on the challenges that had long gone unaddressed, leaving them so dispirited for so long.

The human spark in Bellambi was alive and well.

## WHEN THE HUMAN SPARK DIMS

The problem nowadays, as author Sebastian Junger reminds us, is that we don't place enough value on people's innate capabilities. We are missing something vital in our lives and society. "Modern society has perfected the art of making people not feel necessary," he writes in *Tribe*.[2]

Let me be clear. I am not suggesting that people aren't involved in their communities. Of course they are. We all are. There are countless acts of good works taking place each and every day. This book is filled with examples of them. A big challenge (which I will speak more about later) is how to make these productive actions more visible beyond those people who are directly involved in them.

But I also find we often hold ourselves back from stepping forward, wondering whether we have something of value to offer. And at times, we impede what others have to offer. This is in part the consequence of inwardness. Under the banner of progress, so many of our responses to societal challenges crowd people out. Other times, we seek to mobilize people for protests, marches, or petitions—all fine and good things to do. But there is much more we must do to cultivate our shared lives and build stronger communities together. And while volunteering is vital, so many of us don't do it. Even when we do, it can be limited to a quick one-off event. So much of what we are capable of is being left untapped. To tap our capabilities, first we must value them.

---

2  Junger, xvii.

What gets in the way of any of us stepping forward and leaning into our lives more? Of going beyond a single volunteer experience or signing up for a single march? Of more fully creating the shared values and lives we yearn for? What stands in the way of us recognizing the innate capabilities in ourselves and in others? In our current times, something that appears to be so simple, so intuitive, so basic has become so difficult to pull off. Here are some common reasons.

## We Unknowingly Crowd Out the Capabilities of Others

Well-intended motivations to solve problems lead professionals in a given field, such as education, poverty, and the environment, to believe that they have the sole expertise to understand and act on the problems we must confront. This signals others to stay away. Not just everyday citizens, but other professionals, clergy, and businesspeople, too.

Oftentimes, our actions are deemed to not be valuable by professionals intent on scaling efforts, using best practices, and driving complex processes. These can leave little room for people to exercise their human spark.

In Bellambi, the citizens overcame these obstacles. Different people and groups began to reimagine ways to create opportunity. Only after this shift in mindset were they able to see in one another their innate capabilities. Some could help rid the community of rubbish and graffiti. The police could take action against drug houses. Local residents could come together and revitalize the neighborhood center. Businesspeople could take on job training. Every person in the community was seen as valuable, and they could each do their part to make things better.

We must value the human spark for this to occur.

## We Fear Talking about Our Shared Concerns

In a study I did for the Kettering Foundation, "Will Any Kind of Talk Do?," one of the key findings was the "crisis of self-confidence" we can experience when engaging with others on common challenges.[3]

Doubt kicks in when we believe we don't know enough to talk about an issue or that we'll offend someone by saying something wrong or insensitive. It's the same anxiety you've probably experienced when in a social situation and you don't know what to say beyond small talk.

Time and again I see this doubt and fear play out with heads of local organizations and their staff. You would think that they would be confident in their abilities, but they often shy away from talking with other professionals and community residents, either because they worry they don't know enough about a particular issue or that they'll say something that offends someone else, creates disagreements, or raises tensions. We cannot create shared lives if we do not share our thoughts. We must get past this fear if we are going to be able to do our part.

## We Are Waiting for Permission

I often work with professionals and everyday citizens who are waiting for permission to take action on an issue or get involved in some way. Either they or their group isn't one of the big players in town, and so they yield to others. They'll confide to me that they don't have enough confidence to step forward, and so they wait for someone to signal to them that it is okay to come forward. They're passionate about taking a particular action, but their organization has never done so before. So they wait.

Della Hodson from Bakersfield, California, ran the local United Way. For years, she sought to take on issues of hunger and food insecurity. Kern

---

3  Richard C. Harwood, Patrick L. Scully, and Kim Dennis, "Will Any Kind of Talk Do?: Moving from Personal Concerns to Public Life," The Harwood Group for the Kettering Foundation, December 1996; 17.

County, where Bakersfield sits, is one of the highest producing agricultural counties in the nation. Like so many people, she too was told she wasn't a key player on this particular topic. Nor was she expert enough. When Della and I would speak, she'd worry she didn't have what it takes to help her community move forward. She doubted her own innate capabilities, so she waited for someone to tell her it was okay to step forward.

Della could have remained frustrated and stymied. But she didn't. Along the way, she lost funding and key partners for a different initiative, this one focused on the earned income tax credit. Rather than give up, she found new partners, and together they launched a new approach. Now, the number of low-income people receiving earned tax credits has doubled.

She realized she had more insights, more capabilities, and more unlikely partners from different areas of the community than she could have ever imagined, and she was able to accomplish so much.

Fast-forward a few years. Della stopped waiting for permission to act on food insecurity. She took her newfound confidence and capabilities and built a vibrant countywide coalition on hunger and food insecurity. After that, a major national organization reached out to her to partner.

Our doubts can cause us to step back, step aside, and step away. But you needn't. We must signal to one another that we value each other's innate capabilities.

## We Don't Knock on Our Neighbor's Door

In Winchester, Kentucky, a town I am now working with, one community leader there recently said to me:

> We don't know that somebody's hurting because we haven't invested in our neighbors. We really haven't invested. We don't know they're hurting. Second of all, we're all scared to death to knock on that door because we don't know what's on the other side of that door. We've lost largely a sense of community. If you've lost the sense of community, then how are you going to

*connect across property lines, street lines, neighborhood lines? How are you going to connect with all those people and really invest in them?*

We often become unwilling or unable to knock on people's front doors. Perhaps this is due to a fear of the unknown. What will we find out? What will the other person say? Will we be implicated to take action? All these concerns and uncertainties prevent us from knowing about other people's lives. It prevents us from connecting with one another. It causes our human spark to dim.

Danny Zemel, my rabbi and good friend in Washington, DC, recently hosted a service with congregants of different faiths. Before the service, there was some consternation about whether people's differences would overwhelm the conversation. Will people's unique identities prevent them from finding out what they hold in common?

The service was built around small group conversations, where people talked about their shared aspirations for the country and their local communities. I saw Danny afterward. He rushed over to me, unable to contain his newfound enthusiasm. "The yearning, the deep, deep yearning that people have for meaningful conversations was just so moving and profound. There is such a hunger for it."

True enough. The human spark flourishes when we allow ourselves to discover each other.

## We Believe We Are So Small

There's a conversation that routinely happens with people I work with in communities, such as public libraries, schools, community foundations, and faith organizations. This conversation repeats like a recurring dream. All start in the same way: "But what can *I* do about [insert area of concern here]?" They're usually referring to the toxic public discourse in their community or homelessness, the opioid crisis, inadequate public schools, downtown redevelopment, or some other problem.

Our fear is that the shared challenges we face are too big and daunting for any of us to make a dent in. We wonder if our actions can make any kind of meaningful or significant difference. And these fears are exacerbated by politicians and organizations who assert these challenges can be—*will be*—addressed only through comprehensive, complex solutions that operate at scale. This leaves little room for many people, and so they don't act.

Beliefs that challenges are too big, and we're too small, keep us stuck in place. We find ourselves unable to step over the threshold. Innate capabilities go untapped.

As I've said elsewhere, we must focus on the contributions we *can* make. Recognize that small steps create ripples in all directions. The human spark is about seeing the potential in each person. It is that we each have something of value to contribute.

## THE URGE WITHIN

Each of us has our own reasons, motivations, and hopes for wanting to contribute to our shared lives. Each of us has an urge within us to do so. I believe we are born with this urge. It's innate—part of our DNA.

But there are many obstacles that can stop us in our tracks. Even when we recognize our innate capabilities, we don't always tap into them. Sometimes we fail to see them in others. When this occurs, we miss out on something vital in our own lives—and in our shared lives.

We all live with questions of our own worthiness. We all have self-doubts. All of us must confront mistrust, fears, and the unknown. Time and again, I have had to encourage people to step forward, make themselves visible, and engage. I have coached them to stick with their efforts when they get discouraged, helped them rediscover what they can contribute, and urged them to see what others can contribute. We are not so unlike Moses. Fears and self-doubt filled him, too.

In stepping over the threshold, we embrace life. We are awake. We are present.

We must remember that each of us has these innate capabilities. You don't need a special title, or a specific degree, or a particular pedigree. I have seen this daily in my work in communities by all types of citizens and groups all across the US and elsewhere. Every person has innate capabilities, and we need everyone if we are to make community a common enterprise.

Something incredibly powerful happens when we step over the threshold. We see ourselves as part of something larger than ourselves. We become co-creators of community.

Just when it appears that the human spark has dimmed, or has possibly been extinguished, it is always waiting to be rekindled. Let's pry open room for it, lift it up. Let's speak about it and advocate for it. Let's see it in ourselves and in one another.

## Principle 4

# PITCH A TENT THAT'S OPEN ON ALL SIDES

If there was any doubt about the condition of the community, the high school students in Winchester, Kentucky, left little room for ambiguity. They felt abandoned. They feared being unprepared for their futures—despite attending an award-winning school. Many were being raised by absent parents, some of whom were paying more attention to their drug addictions than to their children. Kids lacked activities, and out of boredom some were turning their pent-up energies to drug and alcohol abuse themselves.

When asked for a town motto, their answers came swiftly. "Get Out!" and "Run While You Can!" These youth felt the community had lost faith in them and had no place for them. The youth had lost faith in their community.

This is in part what I found in Winchester, where Eastern Appalachia meets the Blue Grass region. The some 38,000 people that live in the local area face many challenges. We have partnered with The Greater Clark Foundation, which is working to build a more vibrant and resilient Clark County, where Winchester is located; we'll work with the community over a number of years to help develop leaders, organizations, networks, and a can-do spirit that can spark tangible improvements for the people who live there. Our work began with a report based on conversations with residents and leaders called *Waving the Community's Flag: Winchester and Clark County's Moment*, which included the previous comments from the community's youth.

Upon the release of the report, some adults in town would turn to me in private and whisper: "Didn't we all have such misgivings in our youth?" They'd tell me, "We all disliked our parents, and looked sideways at other adults around us. We all felt disgruntled and disengaged at one time or another. We all pictured the moment when we would escape our hometown to pursue bigger dreams."

But is this really what these youth were saying? Was this actually their story? Indeed, was this what they were crying out for?

Those high school students lucky enough to be mentored by adults in the community said it was the best thing that had ever happened to them. They longed to feel supported and loved. Why should we equate their desire to pursue their dreams with wanting to escape from feelings of abandonment and shame? Surely, being raised by parents more concerned about where their next drug fix comes from, rather than focusing on fixing their child's next meal, is a tragedy.

Every community has its own challenges. They may fear that young people will move away to find opportunities elsewhere, or that their community is beset by gun violence or teen pregnancy or inadequate public schools. Maybe their challenges have to do with racial inequities, racism, and barriers to inclusiveness. There are issues like the loneliness of shut-in seniors. In most communities, many of these issues often overlap.

What are we to do? How can we come together to take action as a community? How can we do this in a way that we productively and positively shape our shared lives? We must make room for the people we'll need to do this. Every person in the community can help. We must bring people together in more effective ways that take advantage of all the resources and talents and gifts a community has.

This is Principle 4: Pitch a tent that's open on all sides.

# WE NEED EACH OTHER

I see opportunity before us, but we must purposefully claim it if we are to effectively address the kinds of issues Winchester and other communities face. There are two intertwined parts to this opportunity:

1. **A deep yearning among people to be part of something larger than themselves.** Amid all the noise and confusion, people want to be seen and heard. They seek to restore a sense of dignity and decency in their lives and communities. We long to build things together and want to be more connected and engaged. In many respects, people feel that they have been robbed of control over their lives, and they want it back.

2. **Solutions to many of our current challenges require marshaling our shared resources.** Children feeling abandoned, the opioid crisis, inadequate public schools, and the like beg for a collective response. No single organization, no one leader or group of citizens can tackle these problems on their own. We need each other.

Here, then, is the opportunity that I see. Acting on one of these factors on its own is not enough. Rather, our task is to actively combine these two elements in an approach of shared responsibility. I believe we can—we must—bring together the resources of our communities in ways that enable us to solve problems *and* harness people's yearning for genuine engagement.

At the heart of this idea is a critical experience I've had over and over again when working with communities. Too often we take action on our concerns in ways that are delegated to and driven by just a handful of institutions and groups. Even when we enlist the help of others, we still only tap just a fraction of the potential of communities. If I had to make a guess, I'd say we're leaving on the table 85 percent or more of our available resources. What's more, so many of those resources involve the time and energy and innate capabilities of individuals and small groups in communities. We are forfeiting the golden opportunity for a community to work together, create together, and achieve together.

I believe we need to take a shared responsibility approach. By this I mean we need to bring together both big and small actions, in mutually reinforcing ways, to tackle our common problems. Everyone must play a part, and we must make sure that every person and every group feels they are invited to join in.

Shared responsibility can get us on a more hopeful path that leverages our collective energies. On this path we can grow our civic confidence and belief in ourselves.

## TAKING A NEW APPROACH

The good news is that organizations, groups, and individuals in many communities are already working toward shared responsibility and making sure those in the community can play a key role. Some have made great progress. Others are just in the early stages.

For example, in Hawaii, I've been working with educators to rethink the relationship between schools and communities. Many schools across the US already have school-community partnerships, but these often take a traditional form. Schools tell partners what they need. Partners deliver by making class presentations or offering student internships. To some people, these are successful joint ventures. In many respects, they are. But for many educators and community members, these efforts are not nearly enough. They want more. Kids need more.

One community organization leader in Hawaii put it to me this way: "We are in it for what's best for the kids in their [entire] educational cycle, not just for a moment. In the world of (some schools) you are trying to pass kids through, or pass them on, to get them off the rolls." She then continued, "As a community organization we view these kids as community members, so we can't pass them on. They are going to be here, so problem-solving is over a longer period of time."

Professional educators in Hawaii, along with other individuals and groups from various communities across the state, say they must shift the focus from producing good schools to finding ways for schools *and* communities to share ownership of public education. In other words, they need to let more people join in the conversation and take action. The goal is to share responsibility for providing their children's education. As one educator said, "It's a big difference from being where we're kind of like doing our own thing, on our own. [Education] should be *everybody's* business."

Despite the difficulties, this alternate route is doable and starting to happen, even if only in small ways. For instance, there are local environmental groups working as full partners with schools to jointly design curricula and teach students. Teachers bring their knowledge about education pedagogy and standards. Community organizations offer deep knowledge of the environment. The new classroom is both inside the school and in wetlands and mountains far beyond the school. The teachers are both professional educators and community members. The students gain new knowledge, inspiration, and mentors—and a palpable sense that the community is *with* them.

What is being produced is not merely an institutional response with the help of the community. It is a community response that involves institutions.

Imagine a whole host of schools, community groups, and community members acting with shared responsibility to educate and rear good kids and active citizens. This is not an isolated school partnership strategy. It is how communities take shared responsibility for their children. This is something we are now working on with our Hawaii partners.

As another example, from an entirely different angle, a major nonprofit in a large metropolitan area has been working with local and multinational corporations to involve their employees in community issues. Their current activities look a lot like traditional volunteer efforts. The nonprofit's staff identifies discrete projects for corporate employees to volunteer for. The companies give their employees an hour or two off to do the projects. Then the employees go back to work. End of story.

We know, however, that some companies see their civic role as much broader. Some want to help build more inclusive communities, lead on climate change, address poverty, and deal with hunger. They see the connection between their business interests and larger community interests. Given their knowledge, resources, partnerships, and employees, they can be productive in partnering with communities and making real social change.

So, in the example, what if the companies and the nonprofit were to take an alternate route based on shared responsibility? What if they both started with a common understanding of the shared challenges of the community that required attention? What if they truly understood the talents, gifts, time, and interests of the corporate employees? And what if, instead of simply plugging employees into nice volunteer experiences, they began to organize themselves to work together, with others in the community, on these shared challenges? Finally, what if they didn't just do this as a one-off event, but they sustained their engagement over time?

As I write this chapter, the Harwood Institute is exploring such a partnership with corporate and nonprofit partners. What excites me is the potential to bring companies into a shared responsibility approach in communities.

In the United Kingdom, there is an entire national, community-based Campaign to End Loneliness underway, bringing a variety of resources, organizations, and residents in communities to build stronger connections between and among people.

The assumption is that only through shared responsibility can a whole community come to know, support, and embrace its community members, especially those who are shut-in. This would first require knocking on people's doors—and dealing with our own fears of what we might find on the other side. We must make room for different people and groups in the community to bring their varied talents and assets and time so that together we can make a difference.

## ON BEHALF OF THE COMMUNITY

This brings me back to Battle Creek, the community in Michigan we had been working with to create a more hopeful path forward. I want to fill in an important part of the story that began long before the launch of the comprehensive change initiative I brought up earlier. It's another good example of shared responsibility taking shape.

Our work with the community first began with six individuals who formed an ad hoc Battle Creek team. Not all of them knew each other. At the time, Kathy Szenda Wilson was from the Battle Creek Community Foundation. Kate Kennedy Flores came from Voces, a Latino-focused, community-based organization. Sheley Bess was an early childhood program coordinator from the Calhoun Intermediate School District and led the local Great Start Collaborative. Matt Lynn and Angela Warren were from the local United Way. Dave Nielsen was a retired educator and active citizen.

When the Battle Creek team attended a Harwood Public Innovators Lab, they assumed they'd identify a community issue, form a new nonprofit, launch a new program, and get a local funder to support them. All this would be done "on behalf of the community."

But as the team did its work, it made a different choice, taking them in a dramatically different direction. Over the next handful of years, they would never adopt any official status, open an office, print letterhead, or even give themselves a name. This was a significant departure from the way things usually got done in Battle Creek.

The team's first step was to hold a series of community conversations to gain a deeper understanding of the community. What emerged was Battle Creek residents saying they wanted more opportunities for their children, more choices for individuals and families to get ahead, and a desire for stronger community relationships.

The community also said it was stuck. People's concerns routinely went unheard. Frustration abounded over large-scale change efforts that seemed to come and go. A lack of trust held back the community. The narrative of Battle Creek also was clear: "We already tried that [fill in the blank]" and "Change isn't possible here!"

The team struggled with what to do with what they were learning about the community. Team members once again felt the impulse to create a new program. But instead of acting on that impulse, they began to wrestle with questions such as what scope and scale should their efforts take? What set of challenges and actions could they wrap their arms around? How could they respond to people's expressions of hope mixed with fear?

At first, it wasn't clear which direction to go. So they turned back to what they were learning from the community. They had been told repeatedly that Battle Creek was awash in programs and new initiatives. People didn't want any more. More than anything, people wanted proof that change was possible. Then the community could build from there. In short, the community wanted authentic hope, not more false hope. This led the team to once more ditch the idea of launching a new program or service.

Then another breakthrough occurred. The team discussed the following important question: "What space should the team occupy in the community?" This question challenged the team to focus on what its contribution should be *in relationship to* others in the community. They reminded themselves that they shouldn't try to be all things to all people and that they (or anyone) couldn't save the entire community, especially on their own.

After much discussion, they made the choice to serve as a convener and connector. Their job was to provide a *space* in which to share with other groups what they were learning from the community and help align and focus existing efforts within the community. What they were doing was to make room for the human spark to take root, grow, and spread. And they did this by opening up more room for different groups to come into the conversation.

# THE RIPPLE EFFECT

The Battle Creek team set out to create real change in the community by making a down payment that change was even possible. And it did so by focusing on the concerns of the Burmese community. At the time, the fast-growing Burmese population was largely invisible to the larger community. Yet what was clear from conversations among residents was that many Burmese shared almost exactly the same aspirations as everyone else in town.

They did, however, face a special set of challenges. The Burmese lacked access to routine health care. Local doctors and nurses didn't know the Burmese language, so things like routine health care or childbirth were much more difficult. While in childbirth, moms were forced to speak over a phone to a translator hundreds of miles away. Or their eight-year-old child was pulled from elementary school to be the delivery room translator.

Meanwhile, children raised speaking their native language at home entered school already behind, and parents felt cut off from local public schools and unwelcomed.

In the team's role of convener and connector, they began to go out into the community to meet with different groups, organizations, and individuals. They never confronted people or laid blame for these challenges. Instead, they shared what they had heard from the community and asked two simple questions:

- What do you make of what we are learning?
- What do you think this means for our community?

Before long, people began to say, "I wasn't really aware of those challenges." Then some would raise their hands and offer, "I could help with that!" or "Do you mind if I invite other people and groups to join our conversation? I think they could help, too!"

This prompted a host of impressive shared actions—each of which rippled in all directions. Dennis Bona, then-president of Kellogg Community College, realized he had programs in health care *and* translation but the two had never been combined. So the college began to train Burmese translators to work in hospitals and other settings. (This ultimately led to creating translators in various languages who came to serve in a host of local organizations.)

An organization that had a mobile primary health care van started to make routine visits to areas where the Burmese families lived. The local sheriff began a training program on how to use car seats for infants; a local toy store provided the seats at a discount.

The efforts then began to spread beyond health care to other concerns and opportunities. Dr. Linda Hicks, then the Battle Creek Public Schools superintendent, wanted to have a deeper understanding of the Burmese culture and community. Through the Battle Creek team, she reached out to the Burmese community, sparking a host of interactions and subsequent partnerships.

One small effort would turn out to be critical. A middle school principal heard that the Burmese community wanted to start a community garden. The Burmese culture is rooted in an agricultural tradition. An available piece of land was next to the middle school, but there was no apparent access to water. The school had water, and the principal offered it to irrigate the new garden.

The community garden in turn produced stronger school-community relationships. It also led to scores upon scores of local Burmese joining in community gardening, and multiple community gardens were started in the community. The gardens then connected to Good Food Battle Creek, where they could sell their fresh produce and the community could benefit from it.

A local Burmese community leader, Martha Thawngmung, led the way to build a new Burmese community center. Out of that emerged a new social enterprise called Unstoppable Noodle. The noodle delivery service employs and trains Burmese youth. To make the enterprise possible, the United Methodist Church makes available its certified kitchen, and Unstoppable Noodle makes use of produce from local Burmese gardens.

An ever-expanding group of community members came together, first in small ways, and then in ways that eventually rippled out in all directions in the community, all with a common purpose. Ultimately, the actions touched on a whole host of community issues and involved a wide array of local clergy, businesspeople, educators, and nonprofits.

What happened in Battle Creek is just an example of shared responsibility starting to emerge in a community. Different resources, from different sources, all came together to move in a common direction.

## WRONG TURNS

My fear is that too many professionals, organizations, and institutions are squeezing out important parts of communities, preventing them from sharing the responsibility of their common challenges. When this happens, we forfeit much of the opportunity present in these communities. We fail to address people's alienation from politics and public life *and* the need for them to play an active role in addressing the issues we must confront.

Now, I can imagine many professionals saying they want to pursue shared responsibility—or even that they are doing so already—only to make wrong turns along the way. There are five common wrong turns worth noting:

1. While there is the desire for shared responsibility, we default to traditional planning techniques that lead to further inwardness. This common mistake leads back to a focus on our own organizations, programs, and perspectives. Meanwhile, we fail to marshal the community's capabilities and resources.
2. In our push for "results," we merely give lip service to engaging the community in authentic conversations. We figure out what results we need, and then "sell" them to the community under the guise of engagement. The problem with this method is that there is little understanding about what really matters to people in communities.
3. Even when we do hold these community conversations, we default

to reaching for best practices that neither fit the local context nor engage other groups and community members in taking action. Decisions and actions remain largely in the hands of a small number of professionals.

4. When we do attempt to pursue shared responsibility, we line up the same groups, organizations, and leaders without realizing that we have fallen back into our traditional relationships.

5. We think about shared responsibility as simply further ramping up individual one-off volunteer efforts to help local neighbors or communities. This is necessary but insufficient when it comes to taking shared responsibility. At issue is how to marshal our collective resources over time, all working toward a common purpose.

I was talking about the challenge of making shared responsibility real with a young professional who recently graduated from a top US university in public policy. At school, he and his classmates were repeatedly told they're the "best and the brightest." Taught, according to this young fellow, to "apply what they learned from a perch atop their castle."

Having a deep knowledge of a community was not on most people's radar, and neither was listening attentively or thinking about what it takes to create shared lives.

We can embrace the language of shared responsibility and still fail to do it. We can continue to view solutions to shared problems in terms of social Erector Sets to be manipulated. Driven by a small, select group of professionals. Imposed by that small, select group of professionals.

At issue is how can we open up a new pathway for communities to forge shared responsibility for their common future? How can a community, such as Winchester, whose children feel abandoned, act collectively to address the future of their youth—and thus their community's future? How can educators in a place like Hawaii forge school-community efforts that in practice reflect a shared ownership for educating children? And how can the major nonprofit work with the multinational company to marshal the collective resources and talents of people, all in the context of the common challenges of the community itself?

The answer: We need shared responsibility. But this takes vigilantly guarding against making the wrong turns on our way.

## RECLAIMING OUR COMMUNITIES

Think for just another moment about the youth in Winchester. Surely, they need good teachers and principals to get good schooling. I can say with confidence that the local school superintendent is working overtime to make this happen. But to genuinely tackle the constellation of factors that are in play, more—*much more*—is needed. The superintendent knows this. Success will take nothing less than a different path rooted in shared responsibility. The good news is that the community has already started down this new path.

In the years ahead, Winchester will need to marshal its resources, from all directions, and from people and groups of all sorts, to help children and the community thrive. In doing so, they will need to work together to generate answers and actions to such questions as:

- Who can mentor, support, and love the children of this community when their parents and families are often absent or unable to do so? And who can support the parents and families to help them step forward?

- What social networks—meaning family, church, and neighbors, among others—can provide the necessary support to help people move and stay off drugs, *and* then to get up on their feet and be self-sufficient? Drug treatment alone will not be enough to give people a real chance.

- What assets do different organizations and groups within the community have to help educate children beyond what the schools themselves can do?

- How might residents and organizations come together—in ways they could not achieve on their own—to get young mothers and families off to a good, healthy start?

- How can the community tackle issues like obesity and unhealthy eating habits—and actually reach people where they live, in ways that matter to them, through messengers they trust?

Not all these steps can or even should be taken all at once. It takes time to build trust, forge relationships, and for new actions to emerge. New people will come to the work when they are ready—not simply when a new project is announced. Strategically, we must start our efforts focused on those things that are actionable, doable, and achievable.

The key is to get early wins in order to build a new, promising trajectory, with growing momentum and ever-expanding civic confidence.

## MAKING OUR WAY FORWARD

My hope is that the idea of shared responsibility becomes a way to seize the opportunity before us, to tap into people's yearning to be part of something larger than themselves, and to marshal a community's resources to address shared challenges.

Shared responsibility is not some new model that must be implemented with rigid fidelity. We already have such models that too often straitjacket communities, siphoning off our attention to implement the model rather than focusing on the community itself. The approach of shared responsibility can be incorporated into many existing efforts.

The starting point must always be what's best for the members of the community and not the professional processes we get so entangled in. Being focused on what is best for the community may sound obvious. But we all know that we get lost in our professional approaches.

People in communities want to be builders, shapers, contributors, and partners. Remember, we must be co-creators of our own lives and communities. This means how the work gets done is as important as what gets done. We must imagine and construct actions that pull unlikely people and groups together, often across dividing lines, often in ways not thought of before, and often with results that not only solve problems but also help communities thrive. Shared responsibility is about a whole host of groups and people having a genuine place in the community. There is a place for *everyone*—from large institutions to small ones, from citizens to clergy, from nonprofits to business. Everyone means everyone.

To effectively marshal a community's resources requires leaders and organizations to recognize and value these abundant resources and how they fit in relationship to them. As such, you must see yourself and others as part of a larger alchemy called community. You must not simply ask, "What is our role?" The better question is, "Where do we fit in the larger community given who else is here?"

Shared responsibility, as I see it, will take different forms. Sometimes it might be led by an organization reaching out to the larger community as is happening with schools in Hawaii. Other times, as in Battle Creek, it might start with an ad hoc group and grow into the larger community. It can launch with a government agency, as happened in Bellambi, and then fan out to include others. It might just take place in a small neighborhood and never spread beyond.

Shared responsibility isn't about seeking to "fix" everything all at once, as if that's possible. Instead, it is about how we tap into our innate capabilities and forge new ways to work together to take shared ownership of our lives and communities.

The truth is that all of these things—in their own ways, at the right times, in the right combinations—are called for, if people are to reclaim a sense of belief and can-do spirit and communities are to solve pressing problems.

> > >

Here I ask you to consider Abraham's tent in the Bible. He insisted that all four sides of his tent remain open at all times. All four sides! Anyone who wished to come in could do so, from any direction, when they were good and ready. They could contribute what they could. The stranger, especially, was welcomed. Even those who were thought not to have much to offer—at least at first.

In our communities, to advance shared responsibility, we need to become tent-pitchers. We need to envision in our minds—and make real through our actions—how we can pitch a tent in which anyone can come in. How can we honor the gifts and talents and resources of all groups, organizations, and individuals? How can we enable people to come when they are ready? How can we create a signal to those who might be resisting change that we will be here waiting for them and will welcome them when the time is right? We become creators when we pitch a new tent and leave all the sides of it open.

There is something basic—*radical*—at the core of shared responsibility: It is relational. Shared responsibility is rooted in a covenant of sorts—an agreement between and among people that reflects a common purpose, infused by shared obligations, undertaken entirely by one's own will. Like all covenants, it calls us to be part of something larger than ourselves, *in service* to something that includes, yet transcends, ourselves.

# Principle 5

# BUILD TOGETHER

Back in 2012, not long after the Great Recession's lowest point of reckoning, my colleagues and I fanned out across the country to talk with people, from all walks of life, about their lives, their communities, and where they believed the country was headed. I've periodically taken trips like this every few years over the past three decades.

On this particular trip, people were largely bereft of a sense of possibility for the future. Their concerns were less about politics and government than about getting back to basics in life. They spoke despairingly about how they were behind on their home mortgages; how they or their loved ones had lost jobs and were worried sick about making ends meet; how the rules of society seemed rigged in favor of the wealthy, connected, and powerful; and how they feared a growing sense of isolation from one another.

As important as these issues were, not one of them topped people's concerns. What did was something so fundamental that we could easily miss it amid all the sophisticated analyses, discussions, and proposals to fix things: how to restore people's belief that we can get things done together.

This sense of belief—this can-do spirit—sits at the heart of the American identity and has since before the nation's founding. Myth or truth, in part or in whole, this idea has long animated the country and propelled it forward. Over time, it has rightly caused us to sit up repeatedly and see our waywardness as a nation, prompting painful struggles that resulted in much-needed course corrections.

I came away from these conversations wanting to know more about what shapes and drives people's sense of belief, especially in these turbulent times, and what it will take to restore it. What emerged is that we must actively imagine ourselves as builders in our communities and the larger nation.

This is Principle 5: Build together.

## RECONCILING THE AMERICAN DREAM

In 2015, I set off on yet another journey across the nation, this time to talk with a wide array of local leaders from eight diverse communities: Baltimore; Chicago; Petal, Mississippi; Sea Bright, New Jersey; Spartanburg, South Carolina; Tacoma, Washington; Trenton, New Jersey; and Zionsville, Indiana.

Each of the leaders I spoke with were working hard to make a difference in their communities—some were trying to improve local education, others were feeding the hungry, and still others were fighting to address issues surrounding race and racism. My hope was that these individuals, whose work is close to the ground, could shed light on the questions I've been wrestling with.

What I found in these conversations is even more important today than a few years ago. The feelings and views I discovered then have only intensified in my more recent travels and work across the country.

My first stop was in Petal, Mississippi, located about an hour-and-a-half drive south of Jackson, the state capital. A local leader said that it felt like a "seismic shift" was taking place in virtually every arena of American life—from the flagging American Dream to the rapid spread of social media to the deterioration of our politics.

By now, of course, these changes are no secret to anyone, but they are worth underscoring here. Many of the leaders I met along the way were deeply troubled by the widening income gap between Americans. Central to their concern was the fading American Dream: While for some people this dream still holds as true as it did for their parents, for many others it is nothing more than a false promise dangled before them.

As one Chicago leader said, "It just seems like the American Dream is actually over and done with and dead. All of the typical traditional notions of the American Dream are over. If you just had a home, you'd be okay. Gone. The idea that if you just had a good-paying job, you'd have it forever and you'd be okay. Gone. The idea that if you worked hard, you'd advance. Gone. The idea that if you have money in the bank, you'd be secure. Gone."

I remember one Chicago leader in particular who recounted her experiences teaching two different groups of college-aged students in the same community and their divergent views on the American Dream:

> *I teach a number of different social work-related classes at a couple of different institutions, and oftentimes, depending upon where I'm teaching, students have different takes on what [the American Dream] means. When I'm teaching a class on a Thursday evening at community college, most students will say that that is a myth because of their life experiences [which have] taught them that the American Dream is for those that look a certain way, have a certain income, have a certain level of opportunity available to them. If I'm asking a similar question at DePaul or at Adler [universities], the answers are much wider in range.*

In my 30 years of extended conversations with Americans, I have almost always encountered people struggling to reconcile the ideals of America with the reality of America. Ideals, though by definition beyond our reach, are something we continually strive for. But never before in my conversations has the gap between those ideals and what we can attain seemed so great. Never before have so many people felt these ideals at such odds with their daily lives and future prospects. And I find this to be the case now more than ever.

A Trenton leader said of the people he works with, "I look at the population that we serve, and they don't even know where their next meal is coming from. They don't even know if their mom and dad are coming home. They're dealing with domestic violence. I mean, all kinds of child-hood trauma."

The divide between Americans can be stark. As one Tacoma man put it, "My reality of what I do, say, and think of America may be because of the real concrete experiences that I have. Not yours. It creates a different reality in America. My house might be on fire, and somebody down the street may be building a new house."

Another example of the destabilizing shifts troubling people is the rash of recent high-profile fatal incidents at the hands of police, which have riddled one American community after another, including New York City, Baltimore, and Ferguson, Missouri, to name a few. These tragedies were brought up wherever I went. As one Baltimore leader put it, "Every-body is waiting for the next Trayvon Martin. Everybody is waiting for the next Eric Garner. And everybody's on edge."

No doubt, in some communities, there's nothing especially new about these challenges. Sadly, they've been part of people's lives for years. What is new is the smothering volume of news coverage that blankets the airwaves as well as social media, heightening the nation's attention and fears. There is an incredible sense of urgency that something must be done.

Wherever I went, and with whomever I spoke, people lamented living increasingly atomized lives. Our politics and public discourse, they said, serve only to further separate us from one another and undermine a sense of belonging. People worry that we can no longer bridge divisions and solve problems.

"It's very difficult to find a reasonable solution because everyone is discussing their own view points and not even willing to say that some-thing on the other side is reasonable," observed one Zionsville, Indiana, leader. Zionsville is a town of just over 25,000 residents located northwest of Indianapolis.

In Baltimore, a leader said that just at a time when people need to come together, many feel on their own, all alone: "There is this lack of hopefulness, which is very, very discouraging . . . There can be a sense of individual survival instead of the collective." This produces an environment in which the focus is on society's negative aspects.

As a leader in Tacoma said, "We have a culture of digging at sores rather than looking for healing." But how do we reconcile the American Dream and begin to heal?

## THE POWER OF BELIEF

In October 2012, Hurricane Sandy pummeled the East Coast, including Sea Bright, New Jersey, where much of that shore community was leveled. People lost power, some lost their homes, and many people lost hope.

But Chris Wood, owner of Woody's Ocean Grille, decided that he and others could do something in the face of this natural disaster. In a municipal parking lot adjacent to his restaurant, Wood rallied locals to bring food, prepare it, and serve it to fellow residents and disaster relief workers so they would be fed and cared for. The makeshift parking lot soon became known as "Tent City," where three meals a day were served, for months.

But neither Wood nor his fellow neighbors stopped there. Sensing there was more to do, they started Sea Bright Rising, a nonprofit that impressively raised over $1.6 million to help people restore their homes and get back on their feet. They got local furniture stores, Home Depot, and others to offer discounts and gift cards. They set up the Sea Bright Solution Center in the borough building where lawyers and accountants and others offered in-kind support to give people a boost.

One Sea Bright leader told me that it was "incredible that people could come together so quickly and provide assistance when they really needed it." But there's even more to this story. Since rallying the community, the leaders of Sea Bright Rising realized that a new phase of work in the community was required.

So, right at the height of their promise, often at the time many organizations would be fighting to grow and perpetuate themselves (which would be yet another sign of inwardness), Sea Bright Rising merged with another group called the Saint Bernard Project. It put itself out of business.

The people of Sea Bright, facing a national disaster, responded in such a way as to strengthen their belief in themselves, but for many Americans such belief in more ordinary times is either fleeting or absent all together. This challenge should concern us all. It can't be left simply to explore in academic seminars or talk shows with political pundits and pollsters. Nor is it something for those running nonprofits and other groups that seek positive change in society to acknowledge and then go about their business without shifting how they do their work.

Without belief, it is not possible to create the kind of society in which we all seek to live. Without having a can-do spirit, change becomes much more difficult—sometimes even impossible—and people are much less likely to step forward and engage with others to find common solutions to problems. And when belief goes missing, people retreat into their corners, hunker down, and fear "the other." Then, pessimism, skepticism, and cynicism win.

Conversely, when there is belief, there is a sense of authentic hope—a *possibility* that something that needs to be changed can be changed. People feel a part of something larger than themselves. There is a greater likelihood that people will see the innate goodness and capabilities in others. When people come together and build, they can achieve things no one individual could do on his or her own.

In Chicago, a leader said to me, "The challenge becomes that more and more people across the spectrum are wondering if [belief] is available to them and, if so, how do they actualize that?"

The key to actualizing something—*anything*—is to make it real in one's life. You must be able to see it, touch it, feel it. It must hold genuine relevance and significance to you. In short, it must matter to you. But how do we make belief more possible and real in a nation of over 300 million people?

The good news is that there is already a foundation present across the country to build upon. Amid all the troubles people see, they find hope in the bright spots they identify emerging from the cracks between society's shifting tectonic plates.

Many point to the Millennial generation—those born between 1980 and 1996—who they laud for bringing new optimism, tolerance, and energy to civic efforts, the workplace, and life in general.

Still others suggest that the spread of social media enables more people to shine a light on problems once ignored and bring many once-unheard voices into the public arena. "Social media is leveling the playing field because it's literally bridging the communication gap across the globe in a matter of milliseconds," a Trenton leader told me. (Of course, this is the important flipside to the detrimental effects of the Internet and social media that I mentioned earlier. Technology is a tool; how we use it determines its positive or negative effects.)

And we must remember, too, that people are working tirelessly on early childhood concerns and health care and other issues in ways that restore belief.

Here's the thing. To get the country on a stronger footing, many more people must engage in ever-expanding actions that bring about greater belief and can-do spirit. But here's the trick. Not just any actions will do.

## BEING PURPOSEFUL

The reality is that a multitude of actions take place every day, in communities all over the world, that help produce better outcomes of all kinds for people, bring greater scale to initiatives to reach more people, and transform the delivery of one service or another. These are all necessary actions that at times make streets safer or provide better schools or even save lives. But if our task is to find ways to engender belief and a can-do spirit between and among people, then there is an opportunity to do something more. We *must* do something more.

My chief concern here is that restoring people's belief and can-do spirit will take broadening our view of the very definition of change and how we think about it. It will require being clear about the purpose and aims of the actions we take. For example, ask yourself the following questions about the actions you are planning on taking:

- Do these actions help Americans reforge bonds of commitment to one another?
- Do they demonstrate that it is possible to bring people together in order to set common goals and set out on a common path?
- Are they catalytic such that if I step forward to assume greater responsibility for my community, others will join with me?
- Do they unleash people's sense of empathy, compassion, and affection for others?
- Do they help pave a way forward for people who fear "the other" to live in an increasingly diverse society?

What all these questions have in common is that they tie directly to the human spark—where *trust* and *relationships* and *moral agency* can take root. Such engagement cannot be contracted out, mailed in, or fulfilled in abstention. Simply solving a problem won't cut it either. There is something distinctly human that people want and need to produce, together, with purpose.

Indeed, when these actions are brought together, they form the very foundation for shared responsibility. When so many people feel so overwhelmed by the difficulties that beset the nation, the challenge is to genuinely draw more people into community and public life, acting in ways that make community a common enterprise and embolden civic confidence.

# REIGNITING OUR CAN-DO SPIRIT

My work in communities has led me to identify five essential truths that everyone interested in moving their communities and the nation forward should use as guideposts to restore belief and reinvigorate America's can-do spirit. The changes people yearn for can be created. We *can* do this.

## People Gain Hope by Seeing Others Working Together

I want to return for a moment to a tendency among those of us who seek to generate change: the growing reliance on the use of data to set targets and measure results. As I have said, there is little doubt that this approach is vital to understanding challenges and determining whether progress is being made. But in the rush to embrace this approach, we must exercise care. Overreliance on the use of data—or for that matter, the urge to reflexively scale different efforts or to adopt best practices that leave out the community or other tactics and strategies—can inadvertently blind us to whether these efforts are helping to generate belief within and among people.

People gain trust and hope by seeing others work together. Think back in American history to such events as barn raisings. The sheer act of building a barn together served as visible affirmation of belief in one another. It proclaimed that we are joined in a common enterprise. It demonstrated that people could get things done together.

I raise this example not to be nostalgic, but to remind us of the nation's rich history and our human needs. A more recent example can be found in Spartanburg, South Carolina, where a group of individuals joined together to launch a community-wide medical equipment exchange, which came to be known as Spartanburg Shares.

It all started in donated space in a local church basement, driven entirely by volunteers, who encouraged others in the community to bring in medical equipment they were no longer using—hospital beds, walkers, even bed pans.

"I felt that it reflected a set of core values that I connect with on a very personal level," one Spartanburg Shares board member said when explaining what motivated him to get involved. "I had a parent who had a preexisting condition, and so she could never get health insurance."

He then connected his personal reasons for involvement to a larger public concern: "I feel really strongly about getting people access to health care and medical equipment. Spartanburg Shares just really jibed with my personal experience and what I felt really mattered." Another board member chimed in, "I guess bringing in the role of faith as well . . . we all come at this from our personal lives, values, from our church experience, and wanting to serve others."

In a study I conducted some years ago for the Pew Partnership entitled *Planned Serendipity*, I found that the most successful community efforts focused on issues that had existing resonance with people.[1] In other words, the issue already had *currency* within the community even if it wasn't on anyone's official public agenda yet.

In addition to whether the issue already matters to them, people want to work on something they can positively affect. This may sound self-evident, but, too often, issues we choose to work on are too big to handle. Efforts stall out. Little progress is made. Enthusiasm turns to discouragement. This scenario happens over and over again in communities. All this does is deaden people's sense of belief, and it stifles their can-do spirit.

But in Spartanburg, the group of volunteers started on a challenge they could get their arms around and achieve over time. "[W]e can see that the work actually makes a difference. Some of the people that come in would have no other way to get equipment to help them leave the hospital. There is a real sense of satisfaction in knowing that you've helped someone to better their lives and to get better," a board member observed.

---

1    The Harwood Group, *Planned Serendipity*, The Harwood Group for the Pew Partnership, 1998, http://www.civicchange.org/pdf/planned.pdf.

When things are working well, there is a response from the community itself. More people see the efforts. In turn, more join in. There's a kind of call-and-response at work. It's a ripple effect in which more lives are touched, and a greater sense of possibility emerges. You can see this in Spartanburg where an expanding number of volunteers have become part of the effort.

There's another call-and-response at work as well—a movement toward reciprocity. "Sometimes when people return the equipment, they will bring something they own. Some other people will give us a cash donation after they bring the equipment back and say, 'You know, this isn't much but I would have had to buy the equipment so here's a donation for you.'"

When people see reciprocity at work, they are seeing the strengthening of the fabric of community. Of course, the provision of medical equipment to people in need could be done by an agency or hospital or some other organization. But these elements of human engagement and bonds of commitment might not be present. And it is this sense of humanity that people are seeking nowadays.

In each of the communities I visited, leaders I talked to reach for examples of people working together that they could see and touch and feel. Ones close to home. In Zionsville, it was their local public schools. In Chicago, people talked of particular neighborhood development initiatives or interfaith efforts.

In another recent study I did with national thought leaders on democracy and the state of America, the examples they pointed out included the number of local food networks springing up in communities across the country, the rapid spread of community gardens, and even *local* efforts to combat global climate change.

What all these efforts achieve is to give people "the opportunity to connect and see our humanity," as a Tacoma leader put it.

## How the Work Gets Done Is as Important
## as What Gets Done

"Any jackass can knock down a barn door, but it takes a carpenter to build one. We don't have a whole lot of carpenters these days and that's part of the problem." This leader from Petal, Mississippi, was making a point that I heard often in my conversations. At a time when so much about politics and community life is about tearing one another down, there is the need to build together.

But it is about more than just getting things done. It is about the ultimate goal we seek to achieve—it is not only about solving problems; it involves building stronger connections and rekindling the human spark within us and within our communities. Thus, the key to restoring people's belief and can-do spirit is that *how* the work gets done is as important as *what* gets done.

Petal, Mississippi, is a small town of roughly 10,000 people just outside of Hattiesburg. I talked with a cross-section of community leaders who had come together to ensure that kids get off to a good start in life so they can develop fully in their later years. Those gathered included a goat farmer who, for many years, has served as a county youth judge, the local public school superintendent, the chamber of commerce head, and the director of a local children's task force, among others.

They each talked movingly about their work in early childhood issues and their proud successes, which included new-parent training classes, reading programs, and, more recently, the acquisition of an old donated school bus that has made their programs more mobile. The brightly painted bus was parked out back when I visited.

But the group became even more animated when the conversation turned to describing how they work together. "The thing that excites me the most is that we have brought together folks from so many areas of our community. It is not just early childhood groups or education groups. We have judges, we have preachers, we have the health department. It's the diversity that has really, really come together," said one leader.

This point, reinforced a number of times in this conversation, as well as in the others I held, spoke to people's desire *and* ability to bridge dividing lines in society.

Another key element in Petal's success is the group doesn't rely on a plug-and-play approach—that is, seeing themselves as implementers of predetermined programs and solutions. In an age of "best practices," this approach can be hard to resist. After all, shouldn't something that worked well in one community be picked up and applied in another? In Petal, they knew better. They chose a different path that more effectively connected them to their community.

Before taking action, they set out to see what needed to be done in the community, weigh the actions they might take, and, ultimately, decide what to do. When looking back on their efforts, one board member described the group's process in this way: "[We had] to determine what the great needs and vulnerabilities of the children and families in the community were, and then figured out how to go about doing something about them."

These group members see themselves less as technical program managers and more as creators of strong children. To do this, those involved in the community must see children in their line of sight, make those children visible to others, and then publicly embrace them. They must be turned outward. Said one Petal leader, "It is not a one-size-fits-all . . . We are producers of great kids."

In this way, people in Petal are making what I think of as a civic covenant with their children. It is a solemn pledge to stand behind kids and embrace them.

As in Spartanburg, the people in Petal sought to build upon their existing assets. Said one leader, "Another piece of the work that we do is built upon existing resources. We're trying to figure out who in this community would be the best person to help us address particular issues." A vital part of how the work gets done is to marshal local resources. This is a modern-day example of people bringing their tools to a barn raising— feeling more included in the work and showing others their own potential.

There's another point worth raising here. It deals with how these leaders and other people bring themselves into their shared space. "One word is *selfless*," pointed out a Petal leader. He continued, "I deal in a world that would ignore just so many people—it is about stepping stones. They are stepping on someone to step up or step over someone."

The Petal efforts, he said, are entirely different: "This truly is community . . . You are not pushing your [own] agenda. You are not here for a selfish reason. There's a need for change; there is a breath of fresh air. I mean, how many places do you go to a meeting and everybody is there again?"

Another leader underscored this point: "There's something very special here. I've never been a part of anything where people park so many of their special interests; where they step out of their silos. There's not as much tension around, 'Here's what we need to do. Well, you know, I can't do that because that will interfere with other things I'm doing . . .' We just haven't had that."

Nor has this group experienced particular individuals or organizations trying to grab credit for the group's success. This is a theme I heard from many of the groups I talked with, and it seems to be brought about, at least in part, by the way in which leadership is shared. "The leadership is very fluid . . . There is shared responsibility and shared leadership . . . how all of that comes together is very difficult to explain and it's something that maybe even defies explanation. But that chemistry is there that allows for a lot of people to get involved and do things and they don't feel that they're out there alone."

Finally, there is one exchange in my conversation with the Petal leaders that I want to highlight. It has to do with how the group intentionally sought to move the issue of the well-being of children from a school district issue to a larger community concern. Here's how they worked in the community after they completed their needs assessment of children, according to a Petal leader:

*It was fabulous for the school district because it took the target off their back. It was like, this is where [children] are when we get them. So it's not the school district's fault, this is a community concern, because this is where children are when they arrive at school. So then you really were not blaming anyone . . . What we're doing is sharing this concern, and the whole reason we're doing this is because we want to figure out what we can do as a community to try to make it better for kids.*

The Petal group is not simply making sure kids get off to a good start. They see themselves as creators of community. During our conversation, one leader made this discovery for himself: "Maybe it's something we don't think too deeply about, but this is community building. People want to be involved with things that are positive and can build their community . . . Something really positive, something neat is coming out of this. When you see those things and realize we're really building roads for the future."

In short, they have been able to regain a sense of control in a world that can feel out of control, chaotic, reactive. And yet, in Petal, they have found an alternate way to move forward. Whether it's working with children and their parents, building a communitywide medical equipment exchange, responding to a hurricane, or creating new community gardens, it is *how* the work gets done as much as what gets done that helps to restore people's belief and can-do spirit. Of course, this means using data and other analytic tools to gain a more complete understanding of the issues at hand and what works to address those issues.

But a central task is to make room for people in communities to work in different ways. It is to recognize that in our current environment of mistrust and broken promises, the rebuilding of civic confidence is essential to strengthening communities and tackling larger challenges.

## Strength and Renewal Come from Being Inclusive

Many of the leaders I spoke with noted that the country is continually renewed—indeed *updated*—by an ever-expanding notion of what it means to be inclusive. Efforts that are more inclusive, which help transcend society's dividing lines, give people a sense of belief and can-do spirit.

One Chicago leader cited the idea that, "History has a moral arc . . . It's long; it takes time. Over time, American ideals have been expanded. The successive generations have given more inclusivity for women, people of color, for immigrants. None of this is perfected, but there's progress and that personally gives me hope."

Local leaders from one community to the next suggested that immigrants have longed played a pivotal role in this regard. In these conversations, leaders often spoke of their family members who had come to America, the risks people had to endure to make it here, and the sense of energy and vitality they brought with them. "My own family, and everybody who I've ever met who came here, had to come here at great personal risk," one Chicago participant said. "They often had to flee here, or they had to risk death or imprisonment to get here. I even have a friend whose parents, on the boat from Vietnam, got caught, sent to jail and the minute they got out of jail, they got right back on the boat and they came here."

Another Chicago leader talked about how the immigrant experience has continually helped to rejuvenate America: "What America has is this constant refreshing. Immigrants coming to this country are optimistic and take risks; otherwise, they wouldn't have gotten here. That constant infusion of this kind of can-do, risk-taking, optimism is constantly refreshing our culture and will keep us leaning towards the optimistic."

Of course, as I write this, the nation is embroiled in a heated debate over immigration. But these conversations existed before debates over a wall on the Mexican border or calls to reshape various immigration policies, which have raged for years. The point of these conversations is that we are a land of immigrants, and that people from other shores have made essential contributions to our ever-evolving nation.

But let's be clear. The benefits of inclusiveness do not derive only from people who have come to this country from elsewhere, but from many others who are already here. These include, for example, young people.

As noted earlier, repeatedly in these conversations leaders hailed the energy and new perspectives that the Millennial generation brings to community and public life. "The curiosity and the freedom that Millennials have, I welcome that as hope for me. They bring to the table authentic conversation," one Trenton leader pointed out.

When I asked about what offers hope to them, another Trenton leader responded: "The Millennials! I am energized by the young people. Not just the young people who are out protesting and all that [but] those who are working the system . . . who are going in and becoming politicians or creating their own businesses . . . going back into the educational system. They're not trying to tear anything down. They're trying to build up. That's where my hope comes from."

When I introduced the topic of belief at my annual Harwood Summit that I convened in September 2015, this concern of who is included in the American story—and how—was raised. The point was made that it is essential to remember and recognize the struggles and pain of people already in the country, and what their predecessors often have had to endure.

For instance, for African Americans and Native Americans, there is a unique relationship to America. Their story is different from those of immigrants who came here in search of new opportunities. Their American experience—often shaped by the need for survival—has been different over the course of time.

In many respects, their substantial contributions to the nation have gone unrecognized and have been undervalued. Their story is a story of remarkable resilience, of continued contributions, and of hope. *This* story is a vital and necessary part of the American story.

Whether it is in Trenton, or Tacoma, or countless other communities, when efforts are more inclusive, when they bring more people into community life, they create a sense of greater possibility. This includes not

just the powerful but also those who have long been outside the rooms of
power—not just those with a voice, but those who have gone unheard. It
includes those with financial resources and those without. It is the inclu-
sion of people who have been left out of making progress that is providing
a renewal of purpose and focus.

And recently, at the Harwood Summit, a similar idea came to the
forefront in terms of being inclusive of people with disabilities. Said
one summit participant, "You could say every new generation creates an
understanding for renewal. You could say bringing in people with disabilities is an opportunity for renewal."

Throughout my travels, community leaders often made reference to
the promise of America and its continual renewal over time. Here's how
one Chicago leader talked about this:

> *This country was founded on a dream, flawed in its realization, but on
> an ideal that we're still striving for. [It] is a country that prizes the new,
> prizes renewal, prizes creativity in a way that's unique. Prizes change in
> a way that's unique . . . Even at an individual level, or at a group level,
> where the shades start to draw and you don't see as much of that light,
> it still glimmers through. It's baked in the cake. It's the soup we live in.
> There's a culture of self-actualization that's prized here, and I think that
> those qualities are unique. Certainly rare.*

Inclusiveness comes in many forms. Sometimes it involves immigrants; other times it is about those who are already here. Frequently, it is
about people who look and sound different from ourselves. It was part of
the story in Petal, where the energy of the group working on early childhood issues was generated by the diversity of its members.

At a time when so many Americans are hunkering down, often in
retreat from one another, renewal itself can come from the very things we
fear—such as "the other." It is in overcoming that fear that the American
promise stays alive and vibrant and that solutions to problems can include
more perspectives and tap into the assets within our communities.

## Change Will Come from within Communities

On April 12, 2015, the Baltimore police arrested a 25-year-old African-American man named Freddie Gray for allegedly carrying an illegal switchblade. Seven days later, he was dead after incurring serious injuries while being transported in a police van. Less than two weeks later, following a series of protests in Baltimore and Freddie Gray's funeral, people took to the streets again, which included the nationally televised burning down of a local CVS pharmacy.

"The death of Freddie Gray opened a wound that had been neglected, had not been treated," one Baltimore leader told me. "The pain in the community, the pain in the city was heightened. There was a fight-or-flight reflex, and the city decided to fight."

Part of that "fight" came from a growing number of people who emerged from Gilmor Homes—the public housing development where Freddie Gray had lived. They banded together to report long-festering health and safety problems. Soon it was discovered that maintenance crews were demanding sex for repairs from Gilmor residents.

This situation makes one wonder how it is that people in Baltimore were able to step forward at a time when it might have been easier to retreat in despair. How is it that the women who said they were preyed upon by maintenance workers now had the courage to speak out? Was this sense of belief among Baltimore residents any different from what I had been uncovering elsewhere in the country?

One Baltimore leader told me that for years many residents had remained silent. "They stayed in the corners. They didn't come out and fight. The bell didn't ring anymore." Now, he said, "Freddie's death rang that bell. Freddie Gray's death rang that bell."

According to a Baltimore leader, one key was the uprising itself. This opened the way for a series of subsequent events, all rooted in people's ability to *express* themselves. "People were allowed to express themselves and I believe hope was gathered from the freedom of being able to rise."

Thus, it was once more the prying open of space for people to come together and see and hear one another that made a difference. It was the nature of human expression that mattered. Here's how one Baltimore leader explained it:

> *What begins to happen is people talk to each other and they can begin to open up in ways that they never have felt comfortable opening up, speaking about their pain and moving forward in their personal lives, beginning to laugh again. Some people, many of our members, just come to the group because of something that's positive that is showing up in a community that has many negative obstacles.*

When this happens, the seeds for belief are cultivated. Here's one exchange I had with a Baltimore leader that still echoes in my mind.

I asked, "Where do you think people gain their sense of hope from?"

He responded: "Witness. Witness."

I replied, "Witness in terms of? Say more about that."

He explained: "They see it can make a difference. There was a time where, this is how it was, this is how it is, and this is how it's always going to be. That was the hopelessness. Now it's, we're tired of that. We aren't doing that anymore. We're not taking it. We deserve dignity."

Something powerful happens when people see and hear one another. When they come to "witness" one another's hardships and pain and struggles.

To witness is to acknowledge, to give credence to—to make real. In Baltimore, like Spartanburg, there was also reciprocity at play, but of a different kind. The gift of seeing and hearing one another. Through their newly discovered power of expression, they came to find themselves and one another.

So, despite the odds, the people of Charm City continue to move forward. For sure, progress is slow, often frustrating, even infuriating. But community leaders there say people are tired of waiting for elected leaders, government agencies, and others to respond. They have come to the point where they believe that they will need to generate the change themselves.

Of course, many people in Baltimore felt let down and enraged when three of the officers involved in the Freddie Gray case were found not guilty, while others had the charges against them dropped. Profound frustration also hit again in Flint as it has suffered through its recent water crisis. But people persevere. They must. We do.

Leaders in each of the communities I visited said that the progress that restores belief and a can-do spirit will emerge from *within* communities where people are able to come together. They don't expect change to come from outside, whether from the nation's capital or their own state capital or from some other external source. Just as in Baltimore, or in Petal, or in Sea Bright, much of this change starts with people talking to one another.

These conversations are generated by local people and groups. Said a Trenton leader, "Government will not create the dialogue. It's a people-to-people dialogue. That's where my greatest hope is."

Untold numbers of surveys and studies have carefully documented Americans' lost faith in various institutions, from government to corporations to religious institutions and more. As one Chicago leader said, "Institutional mechanisms, I think, we've lost faith in. A lot of that has to do with fairness in the sense that it's not working for me and that these institutions aren't thinking about the concerns that matter most to me."

What these conversations point to, however, is a counterforce to that lost faith. Through actions that emerge from within communities, people can restore their belief and can-do spirit.

People are gaining hope from these varied local efforts. It is in the *doing* that this renewed sense of belief grows out of. "There's a lot of people who've implemented things over the last five to ten years that are moving and seeing results and coming up with new ideas and new collaborations and new opportunities to work together," said one Tacoma leader. "In this community, there's more exploration of institutionalized racism going on at the moment. There's exploration of how you hear the voices of community members at the grass roots level."

By starting locally, people are able to reclaim a sense of moral agency *and* responsibility. Sometimes this will be without the help of government, or even in opposition to the government. Other times it will be in partnership with government. Some actions will emerge from a small group of volunteers banding together, such as in Spartanburg.

Other actions will come from a small group of organizational leaders as in Petal. It is not the particulars of precisely who is at the table at the start that matters so much as that the change originates from people within communities.

In Chicago, a leader put it this way: "What I'm really excited about, particularly with the younger generation, is that they're realizing that the system may not fix all this stuff. We're not going to rely on the system to fix this stuff. And we're not going to rely on federal or state level things to fix things. We're going to start locally and push up and do so in a much more systematic way."

The leaders in these conversations agreed that change must start in local communities, in whatever combinations of people and groups ready and willing to move forward. We can build from there.

## The Nation's Rebellious Streak Fuels People's Belief and Can-Do Spirit

Imagine for a moment the following scene: A group of people are sitting in a circle, holding hands and singing "Kumbaya." Perhaps to some people it's an appealing scene, especially nowadays given the growing coarseness of politics and public discourse and people's inability to come together to get things done. This imaginary group conveys a much-longed-for sense of belonging and connection.

Every day, I meet people who are resolutely trying to bring about positive societal change in their communities by driving themselves and others to replicate this scene. But while the niceties of singing "Kumbaya" may warm some people's hearts, it is really the rebellious streak in the nation's history that offers the distinctive energy and drive to draw upon in re-engaging people and deepening civic confidence.

What's "baked in the cake" and stirred into "the soup we live in" is a notion of freedom, one Chicago leader told me. And freedom is a function of American history, however flawed, in which Americans have declared time and again their independence to make a better life for themselves and future generations.

Many of the leaders in these conversations returned to these themes repeatedly in explaining what fuels their sense of belief and can-do spirit.

At the heart of freedom is the desire to claim control and shape one's future. Listen to how this Petal leader described local efforts there: "It's working because we have taken back control of our own process. We are reverting back to more of our independence."

The same themes were sounded in Trenton, near where George Washington once famously crossed the Delaware River, and where one local leader described current efforts in historical terms. "Today's grass roots are tired of the status quo. They're bucking against the grain and they're going against the foundation." He compared these efforts to those of "the forefathers, so to speak!"

The achievements of those that came before us in this country are what people tap into nowadays for inspiration *and* direction. In Petal, when I asked people where they draw hope from, one leader spoke passionately about the rebellious nature and energy that underlay the nation's founding:

> *Go back to the Declaration of Independence. I am proud of that. To me that was one of the greatest periods ever in our country . . . In the Declaration of Independence, we talk about our freedom, but actually it is an indictment. It indicts the British government for harnessing us and using us and taking advantage of us and doing things that no person should have done to another person. We said, No! You are not going to do it any longer. We are free. We believe in life, liberty, and the pursuit of happiness . . . I still think that is a part of our innate being—that we believe that we are free and that you cannot harness us.*

When people reconnect with the rebellious streak of American history, they see greater possibilities for making a difference in their own lives and our shared lives. Listen to this Zionsville leader: "Spirit for me means that . . . kind of burning desire to want to make [the country] better. Our culture, in our country, was founded on that. Throughout history . . . we have to continue to make it better, and I do believe we will *continue* to make it better."

Within the country's shared history, then, resides a belief that when people come together, they can make good things happen. "The grass roots, that's really the key," offered one Trenton leader. "It's not so much that we rely on government. It's within ourselves. It's within our community that we make change throughout the world." Indeed, one can hear, too, echoes of the previous factor discussed, namely that change will come from within communities.

Many people draw a certain get-up-and-go attitude from the nation's rebellious history. A Zionsville leader talked about an ingrained resistance within the country to tolerating a state of prolonged negativity. "We are in a country that I don't think has ever in history wallowed in our own self-pity."

Recall that the pursuit of freedom and independence was what brought the first immigrants to America, and these ideals continue to draw them here. Said one Chicago leader, "Immigrants want to come here and have more liberty and freedom and make a life for themselves." And a Tacoma leader observed, "I talk with individuals who come to this country because we still offer the land of freedom, and a place for free speech where people can express themselves."

A former newspaper editor in Chicago also discussed this idea of freedom, when talking about why so many foreign journalists seek to come to America:

*I was thinking freedom because I recently was with some foreign journalists who were coming here. I wish I would have asked them, "What do you think the American Dream is?" I think they would have said freedom. From their perspective, that's everything . . . The freedom to just report or write on anything you want without fear of imprisonment or death or censorship . . . I think freedom does fuel our innovation in this country. It fuels this feeling that you could start something. When I think of the American Dream, it's always based on the freedom that if you wanted to have the right luck, opportunity, that something magic could happen. In many countries, that just can't [happen].*

Of course, the story for African Americans is different from the immigrant one but still rooted in the pursuit of freedom. In the second verse of the old slave song "Free at Last" are some of the most beautiful words I have ever heard: "I thought my soul would rise and fly." It was an act of faith when they sang these words. It was a desire for freedom and a hope about what might become. This quest for freedom and independence is part of the nation's story; it's our story.

## A HUMAN SCALE

I have already noted that when I crisscrossed the country to talk with Americans after the Great Recession the key insight for me was people's yearning to restore their belief that Americans could get things done together. But there was another key insight that I haven't yet explicitly mentioned: people's urge to take action on a human scale. This notion had nothing to do with what they wanted from politics or government; in fact, many people told me that politics had become increasingly irrelevant to their daily lives.

In many respects, the case I am making about human scale does not solely revolve around government or even making government work better—though it certainly has implications for that. Rather, what people want is to find ways to reclaim a sense of control in their daily lives and to express basic human desires for renewed trust. They want more meaningful relationships. They long to build greater civic confidence.

It often seemed that such human scale action is a prerequisite—some said, a remedy—for putting the nation as a whole on a better path. After all, the more positive actions people can take, the greater likelihood and belief that larger actions are possible.

One story in particular from those post-recession travels sticks in my mind. In Las Vegas, I was with a group of about a dozen local residents and after talking with them for about an hour and a half, I asked the group what they thought needed to be done to address many of the concerns they had raised. A man there told me that he wanted to gather a small number of people to paint a school.

At the time, I recall being incredulous in my response to him: "Paint a school?" I replied. "After all the systemic issues involving education, homelessness, and other challenges that you and others in this conversation have talked about for the past hour and a half, you want to paint a school?"

In silence, he stared down the table at me and then proceeded to give me a firm and clear response. He wanted to gather people to paint a school so that they could prove to themselves and others that they would come out from their homes, set a goal together, achieve something, celebrate their success, and inspire others to step forward. Like in Petal, he wanted to show kids that people care about them and their future. He was saying, "Let's prove to ourselves that we are capable of coming together again."

Each of the stories I heard on my travels across the country holds a similar insight. In Spartanburg, it involved their medical exchange. In Petal, they're getting kids off to a better start in life. In storm-battered Sea Bright, they are literally rebuilding their community. What these and many other stories tell us is that to restore people's belief and can-do spirit, there is a need for more actions on a human scale.

Let me be clear. This is not an argument against a need or desire to bring scale to different efforts, or to measure the effectiveness of our efforts, or to learn from what works in one community and apply those lessons in another. There is nothing inherently inconsistent with human scale actions and any of those efforts. In fact, if anything, what I am arguing for is to make room for more human-scale initiatives as part of that and other work. Let me also say that I am not simply trying to make a case for more volunteering. Revving up the numbers of people who volunteer, however important that can be, will not, alone, meet the test that I am laying out here.

Nor is my argument simply about "small is beautiful," which will not, alone, meet the need for building a sense of common purpose and direction in the actions we take. Nor will it meet the needs for change now required on many issues. Rather, it is how and why people come together that is essential to focus on.

Context is critical to remember in this discussion. People want to restore their belief that they can get things done, together, at a time when they feel seismic changes happening all around them. They've lost faith in various institutions. They are angry about not being heard. They worry that little will result from their engagement. Far too many Americans have hunkered down, feeling stymied. People won't engage simply because we wish for it, or because we raise our voices to implore them to do so. And their engagement won't necessarily stick long term merely because we entice them with some material incentive to get involved.

We need a different approach. Whether we are talking about widespread collective initiatives or small single actions, this new approach will require making room for people and groups and organizations to be genuine parties to change in their lives.

People's shared work must focus on actionable concerns and achievable goals. Grandiose plans and overpromises will only deepen people's skepticism, even cynicism. And careful attention must be paid to bringing people together to erase seemingly intractable dividing lines so often caused by fear of "the other."

What's more, we must make visible those actions that reflect this new approach. We must attach a value to them. We must place them in a larger context of what it means to be an American.

Let's be real. No one believes that the seismic challenges we face today can be solved overnight or even through a series of large-scale initiatives. The task is to demonstrate the nation is moving in a better direction— onto a more promising trajectory. Where the circle of people taking action is ever expanding. Where trust is being rebuilt. And where civic confidence is growing.

This is the path to restoring belief and, ultimately, to gaining the collective confidence that the nation can tackle larger systemic challenges.

# Principle 6

# REMEMBER, COMMUNITIES ARE ALIVE

Not too long ago, I was leading a roundtable discussion with 20 foundation executives about the role of funders in communities. The executives talked proudly about their triumphs as funders in identifying great grantees, underwriting programmatic victories, and solving problems. There were also some reflective moments that bordered on confessions, such as when they spoke about imposing unrealistic expectations for change on communities and investments that went bust.

There was a moment in the conversation when a single word popped up that became a thread for everything else that followed: dignity. Honestly, it's not a word I have heard funders use a lot. Nor do many other people when talking about community. It's a term usually reserved for individuals rather than larger groups of people. That's why I made dignity the theme of the 2017 Harwood Summit, held at President Lincoln's Cottage in Washington, DC.

"Dignity is not really an issue we think of in terms of community," one executive remarked. And then he said, "It's a really big issue. Often, where the community is starting *is* an issue of dignity."

A foundation executive, who was part of a different group conversation, said that funders need to be respectful when working with communities. Of course, dignity and respect are two different things. Respect is earned, usually over time. Dignity is intrinsic to people's humanity.

Dignity is nonnegotiable. It calls upon us to see and hear others. To treat people with inherent value apart from any particular grant proposal or evaluation report. When you afford people dignity, they are *a part of* shaping their own destiny, rather than having it imposed upon them.

When the term "investor" comes up in relationship to communities, you might immediately think of foundations. Many of us do. But we need to expand this idea if we are to create the kinds of lives and communities we want. There are many, many more potential investors in a community. We're each investors in the different roles we play in communities. For instance, I include nonprofits, faith-based institutions, government, and corporations as investors. You can also include local leaders, civic and neighborhood associations, arts groups, and many others, too. I've worked with them all. We need them all. Each plays a vital role.

At issue is how can we effectively invest in communities in ways that honor people's dignity? And in ways that make more room for the human spark and shared responsibility?

A community's civic culture sits at the heart of these questions. It's how communities work and how things get done. But many communities are held back by a weak or even dysfunctional civic culture. Others, at the very least, have a civic culture that *seems* to be working but which must be strengthened if the community is truly to succeed.

But to invest smartly, to be effective, and to approach communities with dignity, we must recognize the very organic nature of communities.

This is Principle 6: Remember, communities are alive.

## CIVIC CULTURE MATTERS

Organizational development specialists tell us that an organization's culture is pivotal to how well an organization performs. Athletic coaches incessantly talk about the "locker room culture" and how important it is to their team's success. When visiting a foreign nation, we reach for books to learn about its unique culture because it is important that we know something about the culture of where we're going before we get there.

In communities, civic culture matters. It's how a community works; how trust and public will form; why and how people engage with one another; what enables change to grow, even accelerate; and how ready leaders, groups, *and* everyday people are to undertake change—and their appetite for it. People's sense of dignity is shaped by their community's civic culture.

In my critique of efforts like comprehensive change initiatives and the use of best practices, I often point out that civic culture is overlooked. These efforts often get implemented with little understanding of or focus on the strength and health of a particular community's civic culture. That's a big mistake. Civic culture is one of the most critical determinants of whether these efforts succeed or not. And whether people feel *part of* their community.

Thirty years ago, when I started out in my career, I didn't have a coherent view or idea of civic culture. It only emerged after lots of work in hundreds of communities. Not all of those efforts were successful— not by a long shot. I gained as much from the setbacks as I did from the successes. Now, after years of learning, this much is clear: Civic culture is critical to a community's ability to make progress.

The very nature of civic culture can be left out of our discussions about communities and our efforts to generate change. At times, the very nature of community itself is an afterthought. Often, dealing with community is viewed as an unwanted nuisance. For many, it's too messy to deal with. It can't be controlled and gets in the way of getting things done.

The truth is that paying attention to a community's civic culture can be the difference between an effort that fails, or gets stuck, and one that generates real results. It's the difference between a community where people are pulling in the same direction or where people can feel isolated.

# MAKING THE SHIFT

On a recent trip to Australia, I brought a new Harwood Institute tool called *The Funders Roadmap*. The tool was created in partnership with the ten20 Foundation, a catalytic funder in Australia. *The Funders Roadmap* is an offshoot of The Harwood Institute framework, *Community Rhythms: Five Stages of Community Life*. The framework was developed over 20 years ago, growing out of our work in Flint. We wanted to know why some communities make progress and others don't. Why some programs or best practices work in some communities but fail to gain traction in others.

The key discovery was that all communities go through stages, and every community is in one of them at any given time. Each stage has unique implications for what's required for change and how change comes about—the capacities a community needs, how fast change can take place, what signs of progress you are likely to see. All these things relate to a community's civic culture. Briefly, the five stages are:

1. **The Waiting Place:** There is an inkling that something is off in the community, but people can't name it. There's no agreement on issues, problems, or aspirations. A disconnect exists between leaders and the community. The community is usually waiting for some leader or group to come to save it.

2. **Impasse:** The community is at loggerheads. There's clarity about "What's wrong," but little agreement on what to do. A lack of trust, leaders, and organizational capacity block a community's ability to get things done. This is often when comprehensive change efforts are announced but inevitably fail.

3. **Catalytic:** There are pockets of change emerging, with new ways of working together. But a lack of trust, leaders, and organizational capacity still plague the rest of the community. A new competition arises between an ingrained negative narrative and a new can–do narrative.

4. **Growth:** There is an abundance of community capacity, networks, and norms for getting things done. Community-wide efforts are making progress. It's often time for larger, systemic change initiatives.

5. **Sustain and Renew:** Clear progress has been made on key issues, but questions about what's next are arising. Often there are underlying tensions on unresolved systemic issues. Tensions between old and new leaders exist. Here, it's time either to renew or fall stagnate.

Strategies for change tend to be sorely misaligned to the stage a community actually is in. Most strategies I see are geared for one of the latter two stages—Growth and Sustain and Renew—where a community's civic culture is much stronger. But the vast majority of communities are somewhere within the first two and one-half stages—including the Waiting Place, Impasse, and Catalytic. In these stages, a community has a much weaker civic culture. Properly identifying what stage the community is in hinges on paying attention to its civic culture. If you can align the right strategies to the appropriate stage, then it's possible to accelerate and deepen progress and help your community thrive.

In producing *The Funders Roadmap*, we turned the stages framework 45 degrees to address the particular needs of those making investments in communities. Just about any group and anyone who has a stake in the health and vitality of communities is an important potential investor.

In *The Funders Roadmap*, we laid out what investors ordinarily do in response to each stage, compared to those activities they should do based on the Institute's research and extensive experience working in communities. We suggested different milestones to look for to determine if a community is making progress. This helps with setting realistic expectations for change and gauging progress.

When foundations, government agencies, corporations, and others use *The Funders Roadmap*, it immediately prompts them to think about community through a different lens—a civic culture lens! This is the point I really want to underscore. They see

- Communities are organic and operate like ecosystems. They're dynamic. They evolve. They change over time.
- Change in a community tends to emerge in a nonlinear way.

- Our efforts can help to shape a community, but we cannot impose our will on it.

- The key is to understand where and how to get started to make change—what's ripe for positive movement. Then, how to actively grow change from there.

- No one organization or leader can move a community forward. Quite the opposite is the case: A collection of organizations, leaders, *and* citizens are required for such a task.

- Shared responsibility must guide action. Different assets must be identified, marshaled, and deployed in intentional combinations.

- We must work with the community, not apart from it.

Seeing a community as an organic system requires making a shift in how we understand the nature of community. Change actually tends to *spread* in a community. It seldom, if ever, happens in one fell swoop by launching a single new initiative or program. Nor does most change come about simply by scaling an effort. Even if you're successful at scaling something—which I hope you are—the overall civic culture can still impede broader and deeper change.

Change builds on itself over time. Much like the actions that took place in Battle Creek—from working on health care issues to education to community gardens to social enterprises. It spreads fastest when we're able to unleash a dynamic that sets in motion a whole set of cascading effects.

As initial ripples of action spread, momentum in a community starts to build. A growing sense of purpose emerges. Public will for working together in new ways grows. The community's capacity for change expands and deepens. A new can-do narrative takes shape.

Over time, you begin to see that a community is able to generate all-important staying power to stick with efforts. Then it has more capabilities to deal with more entrenched issues. And it can use its newly formed capacities to address new issues as they arise over time. The result is short-term wins, longer-term sustainability, and a much more resilient community able to adapt to future challenges.

## CHANGING THE TRAJECTORY

Mobile has the largest school district in Alabama. For years, the schools and community as a whole had been stuck. Even before 1954, when Brown v. Board of Education of Topeka ended separate but equal school policies, the community has been polarized—blacks versus whites, urban versus suburban versus rural, poor versus those with greater economic means.

Some white residents framed the school problems as an unwillingness of African-American residents to improve their lives. Some blacks saw whites as finding new ways to impose segregation.

By 1987, Alabama found itself in the lowest quintile in the nation for per-capita spending on education, ranked 41st among US states. In 1988, desperately trying to get things moving, the local Chamber of Commerce spent hundreds of thousands of dollars for a public relations campaign in support of a local referendum to increase the local school levy. It failed. In 1992, another levy referendum. Defeated. 1999, yet another. It was unsuccessful too. There was no public ownership of the local schools. The community was stuck in the Waiting Place.

Around 2000, the Mobile Area Education Foundation reached out to the Harwood Institute asking its help to change the conversation in the community. Based on the Institute's reconnecting communities and schools approach, an offshoot of the one I talked about earlier that happened in Greenville, South Carolina, the foundation started the Yes We Can! initiative to engage people across the county and spark change.

Our work initially focused on two basic questions: What kind of community do people want to live in? And what kind of schools do we need in order to get the kind of community we want?

To the surprise of everyone, white rural parts of the county felt just as neglected by the schools as the African-American community. Over time, these countywide conversations began to build within the community a sense of common purpose and momentum. No longer was the conversation about people's complaints and frustrations. Now people focused on what they were for.

What's more, new leaders were being identified and developed from throughout the community. Trust was starting to be forged. Small signs of growth in the civic culture emerged.

But then in 2001, the governor sought to balance the state budget by slashing education funds. Mobile would be hit hard. Cuts meant that 300 teachers would be laid off. There'd be a seven-week delay in the start of the school year. All extracurricular activities would end, including a threat by the school superintendent to padlock the local football stadium.

The foundation called for a march downtown. No one knew what to expect. Foundation leaders feared no one would show up. That day, 10,000 people filled downtown streets, which prompted the foundation to speed up the Yes We Can! effort, holding even more conversations, developing more leaders, and generating greater public interest. Eventually, the school superintendent and the school board became invested. Emerging from these varied efforts was a new community covenant in which schools and the community took shared responsibility for moving forward.

Then what was thought to be the impossible happened. The first school levy in 41 years passed!

New results started to slowly emerge, one building on the other. Reforms included new STEM curricula. New incentives were put in place for teachers to work at lower-performing schools. Scores for 3rd grade-level reading shot up. The so-called achievement gap closed.

In 2001, only 27 out of 101 schools in the district were meeting state standards. By 2004, it was 42 out of 101, and by 2005 it was 61 out of 101, with many of them exceeding the standards.[1] In 2011, 9 out of 13 Alabama schools awarded the Torchbearer award for highest-performing, high-poverty schools in the state came from Mobile.[2]

---

1   "A Report to the Mobile County Community on the State of Public Education," Mobile Area Education Foundation, 2006, http://www.yeswecan.org/pdflinks/report.pdf.

2   Rena Havner Phillips, "Mobile County Leads Pack, with 9 of 13 of Alabama's Torchbearer Schools," AL.com, November 15, 2011, https://www.al.com/live/2011/11/mobile_county_leads_pack_with.html.

In 2011, another school levy passed—this time, with 87 percent of the vote.[3]

Carolyn Akers, the inspiration, force, and drive behind the Mobile Area Education Foundation, said that through Yes We Can!, "We created hope."

When I recently visited Montgomery, Alabama, to keynote an Alabama Association of School Boards conference, I was told progress in Mobile continues, notwithstanding persistent challenges. Folks there keep working at it. A community that for years was stuck in the Waiting Place has moved well into, perhaps beyond, the Catalytic stage. It simultaneously has made progress rebuilding its civic culture as it brought about changes in education. This is an example of what happens when you keep in mind that a community is a living thing.

## INFUSING LIFE INTO A COMMUNITY

There's actually a set of factors that help to create a community's civic culture and propel the community forward. You can proactively invest in these factors. My argument is that we *must* invest in them if we want to make community a common enterprise.

The factors include supporting local conversations and research on local issues; helping to build networks for innovation and civic learning; developing local leaders and change agents; building outward-facing organizations; opening spaces for community discussions; creating shared norms for interaction and engagement; and catalyzing small-scale actions to build momentum, among others.

By developing these factors, people are able to find a place for themselves in the community. They are able to engage with others, solve problems, and build together. By operating in authentic ways that produce sound relationships and results, organizations and leaders generate trust and authority.

---

3  Renee Busby, "Mobile County School Tax Renewal Appears to Pass Easily," AL.com, March 23, 2011, https://www.al.com/live/2011/03/mobile_county_school_tax_renew.html.

In time, a community begins to see that it can move itself forward. Civic confidence grows. The community comes to know that it has its own assets, experiences, know-how, and wisdom to tap. Community norms transform—how people talk to each other, interact, and work together improves. And people's expectations of themselves, each other, and the community grow.

There's nothing magical here. It takes hard work and persistence. And it takes making the right investments.

## AREN'T I ALREADY DOING THIS?

You may be wondering, *But aren't I already doing all this?* I hope so. But just for the sake of clarity, I'd like to take you on a quick tour of some of the wrong turns people make when seeking to invest in their community's civic culture.

Missing from various activities is a clear reference point for how communities operate, change, and evolve. When this larger frame goes missing, the following happens:

- We think developing a sound program or initiative is enough. But really we want to be designing efforts that *simultaneously* build the civic culture of a community.

- We do leadership training that focuses, say, on conveying important data about the community, offering opportunities for people to make new connections and learn about good governance policies. All good things to do. But an entirely different approach is required to think about developing leaders who can work effectively within the organic nature of a community. This requires a deeper understanding of how communities work, how change unfolds, and how they need to adapt over time.

- We build the capacity of organizations so they have sound financial systems, strong employee policies, and good governance structures. That's not the same as developing organizations that are turned outward and that know how to build the civic culture of a community as they do their strategy and programmatic work.

- We undertake "civic engagement" to hear people's voices so they feel seen and heard. But do their voices actually inform strategies?
- We say we want people to help support change in communities. But are community residents active builders of their communities?
- We align different organizations to work together. But it is another thing entirely to marshal the resources of a community to embrace shared responsibility.

I'm trying to draw clear distinctions between what I am suggesting and what is often done in communities. My goal is not to disparage anyone's efforts. Nor is it to minimize them in any way. I know how hard this work is. But getting to the real change we seek will require us to invest in new ways in our civic culture.

## RETHINKING THE RELATIONSHIP

An hour was the entire amount of time required for the Australian funders to begin talking about communities as organic systems that evolve and change over time. There was nothing magical about this shift. As soon as I introduced *The Funders Roadmap*, the conversation took off in a new direction. Those in the room began to see implications for their efforts and how they must change their posture toward communities. And I have seen this dynamic work in other places too, like Battle Creek, Flint, Mobile, and elsewhere.

I can also tell you that I've followed the work of funders in Australia after these *Roadmap* conversations, just as I have in working with people in the US and Canada, and I can verify that their progress did not end with the conversation. It continues on—whether it's a funder working with a small indigenous community, another seeking to work nationwide, or others pursuing change in various communities and regions. The shift made during that initial conversation has persisted in bold ways.

The importance of the radical nature of this shift cannot be overemphasized. One funder put it to me this way: "We must learn how to sit at the table as a respected and valued partner and think about how we can add value by not just leveraging our money."

This clearly requires that you think about investment differently. No longer can it just be about money. In different ways, in different stages of community life, there is an array of investments that can grow a community.

When you are able to make this shift, you will feel liberated. Many people talk about finally feeling a sense of "permission" that it is okay to start with smaller actions and build up. They often embrace a corresponding sense of accountability—even if we can't change the world, we must be clear on what our contribution is.

When you have these conversations, you see that you must work *with* the community, as opposed to *apart* from it. The idea of change happening *over time* becomes critical. And it's possible to see that your existing actions may be even undermining a community's ability to move forward.

A government agency I was working with realized that they were pumping too much money into a community, when other investments like hearing the community's voice and developing leaders and organizations to support change would have been better. Or I've seen foundations recognize that their investments don't align with the community's own aspirations and concerns. Thinking about civic culture requires you to fundamentally rethink your *relationship* with your community.

## PLACE PEOPLE AND COMMUNITIES AT THE CENTER

I continually wonder what separates those investors who place people and communities at the center of their work from those that don't. I don't necessarily think of this question as having a clear-cut, simple answer. There are many shades of gray. I do believe, however, there are some distinguishing features, and these qualities are human in nature. To continually remind ourselves that communities are alive we must value their dignity and realize that they are organic.

## Value Dignity

Your work and the relationships that shape that work must be driven by the importance of the dignity of people and communities. You must genuinely have people in your line of sight. You must see and hear them. Your efforts must include people in helping to build the community in which they live, not merely be passive bystanders, or recipients of services. It means that you know that communities are owned by the people who live there.

Lifting up dignity means that in places like Australia, there is an understanding that indigenous communities have repeatedly been acted upon by outsiders descending upon their communities with pre-set solutions that bear little relationship to their culture, people, or aspirations. Sadly, the same can be said of what happens in many American communities and elsewhere.

The role of dignity—not mere respect, but dignity—calls us to take a different path. Civic culture is about the community's norms, how people interact and engage, how leaders and organizations operate.

## Realize Communities Are Organic

You must shift how you think about the very nature of community. Communities are evolving organic systems that can be shaped but never controlled. They are living, breathing entities.

Thus, strengthening a community's civic culture is imperative. It's what allows the organic system to function. Knowing that change occurs only over time is essential. All this can lead you to reimagine the nature of your opportunity for investments, who and how you partner with others, and how you measure results and learn from your efforts along the way.

This shift will not only transform your practices, but your relationships with your community.

Let me be clear. Taking on one critical element without taking on the other is necessary but wholly *insufficient*. Achieving either shift is not automatic. Achieving both is something to write home about; it's what you should strive for.

It is probably most accurate to say that the investors I have found making the most progress on these two critical elements see their efforts as an expedition of sorts. It's like you're climbing a mountain or going on a strenuous hike or traveling across the country. The process is to take two steps forward, and inevitably fall back, only to push ahead again. But you must persevere, persist, and keep going, like all good things in life.

# GROW OUR CAN-DO NARRATIVE

One afternoon, I got an unexpected call from a local foundation president in Youngstown, Ohio. He asked me if the Harwood Institute would engage the community there on education issues. The governor had taken over the public schools and appointed an Academic Distress Commission to figure out how to raise community expectations for public education. The way the story was relayed to me was that just when the commission was about to publicly release its recommendations, it realized the broader community had never been engaged.

Such a failure on such a vital issue isn't unique to Youngstown. It happens all the time, in communities everywhere. When I tell this story in speeches, I often ask audiences if this situation sounds familiar. They always let out a knowing laugh, as if to say, "Yep, as crazy as it sounds, I've experienced that, too!"

I told the foundation chief the Institute would come to Youngstown under two conditions. I get to decide who we talk with. And I get to choose the questions we ask. He agreed.

We teamed up with a variety of local organizations and groups to pull together conversations with community residents, teachers, and youth and to do in-depth interviews with local leaders. Based on these discussions, a set of critical insights and recommendations were later released in the public report, *The Right Relationships and Conditions to Achieve High Expectations.*

But as we engaged the community, a disturbing narrative emerged about how adults in Youngstown viewed youth. Here's a few examples of the kinds of things we heard:

"When we see kids in Youngstown walking down the street toward us, we move to the other side of the street."

"The kids in this town are up to no good. Many will end up behind bars."

"When we look into their eyes, we do not believe they have the potential to learn and succeed."

We then talked with young people in town. After about an hour of conversation, they would say, "We know what the adults in this town say about us. We hear it. We feel it. We see it!" Here's what the youth told us:

"When they see us coming down the street, they go to the other side."

"When they look at us, we can tell they don't believe in us."

"They think that all of us are up to bad things."

Think about it. Here's a community that has set out to raise expectations for student achievement, and this is the story people tell about their youth. And the youth were fully aware of it. How can a community expect to accomplish anything with such negative beliefs about the very kids whose lives they are trying to improve?

Any community's ability to move forward hinges on the story people tell one another about themselves and their community. To make progress, it's critical that we focus on creating a can-do narrative.

This is Principle 7: Grow our can-do narrative.

## THE IMPORTANCE OF THE NARRATIVE

These narratives drive our individual and collective mindsets, attitudes, behaviors, and actions. They shape how we see ourselves and how we see the larger community. They signal to us what is possible—and what isn't. In Youngstown, the narrative forged a tight grip on the community, reinforcing a self-fulfilling storyline of resignation, defeat, and negativity.

Community narratives are like the personal stories we each carry around. These are the tapes that play over and over again in our minds. Often negative, they can nag you, pull you down, and preoccupy you. Many come from your childhood and others come from important life experiences. Do these sound familiar?

- I am not capable of doing that.
- No one will support my new effort.
- I am not worthy.
- I am overweight or not good-looking enough.
- I will be bullied if I speak up.

For me, personally, it's, "He's a Lemon." This narrative follows me in spite of my work achievements, building a family, having a healthy marriage. Shaking these stories is hard.

Much like for each of us as individuals, every community has its own distinct narratives that it tells itself. My experience is that in many communities—most communities—there's some form of an ingrained negative narrative. Perhaps it's "We tried that before; it'll never work now." Or, "We're just waiting for the next mayor to get elected, and then everything will get better." Or, "No one ever wants to get anything done around here."

I worked in Las Vegas during the mid-2000s at the height of their economic growth. At the time, the community's narrative went something like this: "I'm for me, and you're for me!" Most people who live in Vegas moved there from someplace else to pursue their last best chance at achieving their own individual American Dream. During the economic expansion, many people had put on blinders, focused on their own lives, and made their own way forward.

The community's bravado produced a belief that any challenge could be overcome. All it took was a few leaders getting together and taking care of it. The Harwood Institute documented all this in a report called *On the American Frontier*.[1]

The Vegas narrative left little room for a sense of connection and belonging and saw little use for community as a common enterprise. So despite the community's belief that it could overcome any challenge, at the time it was plagued by inadequate public schools, persistent water shortages, and homelessness. People told us that the community was starting to suffer from having too much of a good thing. The "me first" narrative was preventing the community from generating a sense of common purpose and the needed public will for action.

Not until the Great Recession hit, and the mortgage crisis leveled Las Vegas, did the community come together in new and more constructive ways.

## INGRAINED NARRATIVES

A community's narrative (or narratives) is not difficult to hear if you listen closely to people talking about their community. Ingrained narratives frame how people see things, the actions they take, the ways in which they relate to others, the ideas and thoughts they are willing to entertain and even support. People's sense of possibility and hope are affected by these narratives.

When ingrained negative narratives are in play, they can lead us to believe certain things about our community that can prevent or stall local efforts:

- We believe people really don't care about the community or one another.

---

1    Richard C. Harwood and Jill C. Freeman, "On the American Frontier: Las Vegas Public Capital Report," 2004.

- We choose to forego genuinely engaging people to understand their concerns and take part in the community's work—assuming they have nothing of importance to say or offer.
- We say all leaders are out only for themselves, so we tune out genuine calls for action.
- We approach change efforts with the idea that results are unlikely, and thus fail to stick with efforts when encountering difficulty, or even choose never to get new ones underway.
- We come to fear "the other."

Ingrained narratives can cause us to resign ourselves to a negative view of our community, society at large, and to the very nature of each other. Any notions of change can appear to be too heavy a burden to lift. The levers of change can seem too distant and beyond our reach. People then make offhanded comments that they may not even realize are cynical and mistrustful in nature, and a toxic negativity spreads. Like it or not, these ingrained narratives seep into our thoughts, consciousness, and actions.

## THE ROLE WE PLAY

Think about the times you've been with friends or colleagues when you begin complaining about elected officials; questioning whether some project in your community, neighborhood, or place of worship will ever work; or if people in the community actually care about one another. A groupthink emerges that takes on a life of its own. At times, this can offer us comfort, soothing our anxieties or anger. It allows us to feel part of a group, and prevents us from having to take ownership of what's around us.

Sometimes, in these situations, we can make room for something constructive to flourish, but all-too-often we squeeze out this possibility. How often does such an ingrained narrative make you feel indifferent toward your community or to others? Where you might throw up your hands in frustration, perhaps disgust, and walk away? Where you choose to stand apart from the community and those in it, rather than to see yourself as part of it?

After I tell stories like the ones from Youngstown and Las Vegas in speeches and meetings, people from other communities will come up to me afterwards to tell me their own personal accounts of ingrained narratives from their community. These are powerful stories. Perhaps because they almost always deal with our human condition and inherent longing for a sense of possibility and hope.

There is often something else at work just beneath the surface of people's stories. They want to tell me something that sits deep within them. A kind of personal confession takes place. They, too, it turns out, have fallen prey to spreading negative stories of ingrained narratives. It troubles them as to why they do this. Instinctively, they know that such negativity holds their community back. More profoundly, they know that it holds them back.

The reality is that each of us, in our own lives, in our own ways, pass along these ingrained stories from one person to the next. These narratives are disheartening and insidious. They signal to people to not come out from their homes and engage with one another. "Stay behind your threshold," they whisper to us. They tell us that various actions will not lead to anything, suggesting to people that they ought not to risk trying because they will fall short.

At a time when we so desperately need one another to step forward, make ourselves visible, and engage, these narratives tell people to retreat, hunker down, and succumb to fear.

## CIVIC PARABLES

These days we need a new can-do narrative that helps us feel we are on a more promising trajectory, with growing momentum and expanding civic confidence—that signals to us that we need not succumb to fear. We can build together.

Telling what I think of as civic parables is essential to making the shift from ingrained negative narratives to can-do narratives. All parables have a moral or lesson embedded in them. That's one of the things that make them so compelling. They implicate the reader or listener. Consider the example of the Good Samaritan parable.

As you may recall, it's the story of a man walking along a path who is knocked down and robbed. Then along comes a high priest who sees him on the ground. The person we would expect to stop. He's a leader in the community. He's someone with resources. But, what does he do? He bypasses him.

Then another individual comes along. Someone else we'd expect to stop, but he also goes past the man who has been robbed and hurt.

Finally, the Samaritan comes along. The person from "the other side of the tracks." Now, he's someone lacking in resources. Here is an individual who many might expect not to stop, but not only does he stop, he also helps the injured man to his feet. Not only that, he walks the man back into town. And he doesn't just leave him there. He finds him medical attention. Then he waits to make sure the man is okay and back on his way.

The power of this parable is that it teaches us that one day we could be any one of those actors in this scene. The individual who was knocked down and robbed. One of the people who bypassed him. Or perhaps we can be the Good Samaritan.

The parable teaches us that we have a choice about how we engage with others. It reminds us that the labels attached to people cannot predict what they will do. Nor the innate capabilities they hold.

A good parable helps us to see ourselves in the story and lets us see a way to take action on the lesson it teaches us. It engenders a sense of belief about what is possible. It engages our imagination.

In Flint, years ago, we had teamed up with our partners there to collect a series of civic parables from across the community to help spark people to re-engage and reconnect after years of negativity, division, and finger-pointing in the community.

Fannie Odom, an older Flint resident, shared this story: "We all see empty lots around town and none of us like it," she said. "They weren't lots anymore. They were dumps and had been for years." The lots were such a mess that folks went to Flint's community foundation and got a grant to clean up the trash, and, after four months of delay, finally got the city to haul all the trash away. Then, Mrs. Odom and others in the neighborhood created community gardens in the cleaned-up lots. Now, even children are in on it. "They're city kids," Mrs. Odom said. "They never had a sense of planting anything. The kids would say, 'We'll never get anything to grow here.' I said, 'Honey, you have to have confidence.'"

This story is easy to relate to. Maybe we won't start a garden on some empty lot. But maybe, just maybe, there is some other action we might take. More than anything else, people want to be able to see themselves, hear themselves, and imagine themselves in their community narrative. The right stories can prompt us to take a step forward. They can reignite our human spark.

## QUALITIES OF CIVIC PARABLES

What all civic parables have in common is that they provide a civics lesson of sorts and a sense of possibility. They tell us that anyone and everyone in a community is an actor, a shaper, a builder of our shared lives.

Interestingly enough, these stories are *not* intended to give people answers. They offer us insights. They guide us. Inspire us. Call to us. Beckon us. We are summoned to respond.

The power of a parable's essence is that it can apply in different contexts, by different people, at different times. The story reveals something universal that people can take with them and make their own. They are reminders of who we are, who we have been, and who we can still become. There is a set of characteristics that I have found define a good civic parable. They are rooted in reality, bring us on a journey, help us see choice, make an entreaty, and give a sense of possibility and hope.

## Rooted in Reality

Civic parables are never divorced from reality or sugarcoated. Their very currency comes from being rooted in people's individual *and* collective lives. The real challenges we face. The emotions we feel. The hurdles we must overcome. It is by being rooted in reality that the story holds meaning and is meaningful. It speaks to us, where we are.

## Bring Us on a Journey

Civic parables describe a journey people take together to act on shared challenges they face. These stories bring life to where we may have fallen down, made missteps, or failed and how we got back up and moved on. These stories resonate because they put basic human trials alongside small steps of progress. They help us to gain a new sense of possibility, and not to fear or seek to sidestep failures along the way.

## Help Us See Choices

Civic parables are built around the choices people make, the tensions they encounter, and turning points in their journey. They help us to see how change comes about. They help us to discover what would have come from inaction.

## Make an Entreaty

Civic parables are an invitation—for listeners to engage, step forward, take action, and create their own story. This happens both as we hear about others who have stepped forward and also in terms of what we can imagine doing ourselves. Entreaties are different than shouting at people, attempting to make people feel guilty, or inflaming people's anger. They are invitations to join in *creating* something.

### Give a Sense of Possibility and Hope

The test for civic parables is not whether they reassure people that things are great or even that everything will be fine. Instead, these stories leave us with a sense that we can come together with others to create change. It is possible for tomorrow to be better than today.

When I think about ingrained narratives, I always remind myself that we each have a choice about how we engage with others and how we lean into our own lives. We can be passive bystanders or become builders. We can pass along more negative stories or seek to focus on productive efforts.

You have control over the stories you tell. You have a choice about what you bring to life, what you pass along, what you make the focus of our shared narrative. This is not without challenge or risk, but fundamentally these are our choices to make.

## DON'T JUST SAY: DO

When people hear me talk about the need to replace negative narratives with can-do narratives, their default modes take over. Immediately they equate the need for a can-do narrative with launching a public relations or traditional communications effort. They want to hang banners from street signs and flood the community with feel-good stories. But such actions won't work. People don't want to be sold another bill of goods. This only creates more false hope.

What's more, the remedy is not simply to barrage a community with *more* stories. Good and timely storytelling is always important. But just ramping up the number and volume of stories will not turn around an ingrained negative narrative. It's the equivalent of assuming that merely by raising the volume of debate we will improve its tone and substance. More is not always better. Sometimes it just creates more noise and confusion.

Another trap you can fall into is to ramp up stories about your own organization or group, touting your successes and impact. When I work with various groups, I often ask them about whether they are telling stories about the community's progress. They almost always assure me that they are.

Then I ask them to show me their websites and promotional materials. Inevitably, what I find is that these groups are telling stories about themselves and their own programs and initiatives. Nothing is wrong with that. All organizations and groups need to position themselves. The problem is that by putting your organization at the center of the story you crowd out the community. You would be better served by focusing on the community effort, with your organization as one actor in the story.

## KEEPING IT REAL

I've seen lots of communities make an intentional shift in their narratives. Take Battle Creek. The six people we started our work with years ago created *The Battle Creek Fable* as a way to tell the new emerging story of the community. It was a story that they had written and then simply made copies of and passed around to others in town.

*The Battle Creek Fable* first came about when the team was struggling to find a way to talk about the progress being made by the community. The fable sounds like a Dr. Seuss book. In the excerpt that follows, notice its civic parable qualities:

> *For many years the leaders of the Battle Creek community; civic leaders, business leaders, government leaders, corporate leaders, non-profit leaders, had been trying very hard, with the very best of intentions, to make their community better.*
>
> *So, one day one of the leaders said, "I know what our community needs."*
>
> *Then another leader added, "I have a plan to meet that need."*

*Then a third leader joined in and said, "I have a program to make that plan work."*

*And they tried, and they tried, and they waited, and they waited.*

*Soon after, another leader said, "I know what our community needs."*

*And yet another leader added, "I have a plan to meet that need."*

*Then one more leader joined in and said, "I know a consultant with a program to make that plan work."*

*And they tried, and they tried, and they waited, and they waited.*

*All the while small voices in the community could faintly be heard, saying,*

*"I need help,"*

*"I don't know what to do,"*

*"I have something to say,"*

*"No one is listening to me."*

*So another leader said, "I know what our community needs."*

*And another added, "I have a plan to meet that need."*

*And a third added, "I have a program to make that plan work."*

*And they tried, and they tried, and they waited, and they waited, and there they stayed, sitting in that waiting place, hoping for the changes they sought, and nothing happened . . . nothing changed . . .*

*. . . Until some people in the community stood up and shouted,*

*"STOP!"*

*"ENOUGH IS ENOUGH!"*

*"WE NEED SOMETHING ELSE!"*

*And so, groups of people began listening to those small, concerned voices. They began engaging the community in conversations, asking them what they wanted their community to be. They began listening to the aspirations people had for their community, and this is what they heard . . .*[2]

---

2   Richard C. Harwood, "The Ripple Effect: How Change Spreads in Communities," The Harwood Institute for Public Innovation for the Kettering Foundation, 2015, https://www. thepattersonfoundation.org/images/initiatives/aspirations-to-actions/The-Ripple-Effect.pdf.

Dave Nielsen, a Battle Creek core team member, and a main writer of this fable, summed up the impact of writing it: "It had a tremendous effect on us. In a fairly dramatic way, it brought to light all the things that hadn't worked out in the community and really cemented our commitment to a new process that we were confident would work out."

New chapters of *The Battle Creek Fable* were written every six to nine months. The very process of writing these installments created a much-needed mechanism and discipline for the team to pull together what they were seeing and learning in the community and to make sense of it all.

The team also discovered that the fable was one of their most powerful tools for spreading change in the community. The team tapped into its diverse set of networks to generate and share the fable. Sometimes they shared it in its entirety, other times in part. Sometimes they shared it informally, other times formally. Sometimes it spread organically from one person to another, other times through more organized efforts.

In whatever form, *The Battle Creek Fable* helped to create a common tale of the community, the shared work people and groups were producing together, and the emerging changes taking root.

By writing and releasing the story in chapters, as the ripples in the community unfolded, it signaled that there was no final act or ending to the story. Instead, the fable served to illuminate what was possible. It implicated those who heard it: You are needed to help write the rest of story of the Battle Creek community.

Many of the people we worked with in Battle Creek continue on in their efforts. For sure, there have been ups and downs and struggles. But the new can-do narrative that emerged from those earlier times has helped the community continue to move forward.

## MAKING IT HAPPEN

Those of us interested in giving rise to a new can-do narrative must be prepared for a sharp and long-term competition between the new emerging narrative and a community's ingrained negative narrative. The latter does not give way easily. This is a fight to redefine what a community is and what it seeks to become.

And these new can-do narratives cannot be imposed on a community. They only *emerge*. The stories bubble up from within a community, reflecting genuine efforts of progress and new ways of building together. Think of these as new proof points of a better direction.

For these stories to emerge, you must first find them and make them visible. So many of the good and productive efforts taking place in communities remain invisible to most people, other than those directly involved in them. Greater emphasis must be placed on discovering and highlighting these stories.

Then you must start to actively spread the stories. These stories, or civic parables, make their way into and through the community by word of mouth and careful communications approaches. You must maintain their authenticity by not embellishing them, washing them clean of where people failed or fell down, or by pretending that the actions being highlighted solved the entire problem at hand.

A new narrative can only unfold over time, giving people a sense that a new trajectory is at work. Time is a critical dimension here, because people must be able to see where they are, what came before, and the hope for the future.

And a new narrative only takes form when people can see and make sense of the connections between and among different stories. This is what creates a *believable* track record. It's what creates a sense of coherence and meaning for people.

The prevalence of negative narratives in our society makes it all the more important for communities and groups to focus on creating a can-do narrative. Without this, communities will remain stuck, endlessly telling and retelling stories that undermine their ability to move forward. And our country will remain stuck, too.

Ask anyone about their lives, their community, or anything they value, and they will likely respond with a story. Seemingly disparate pieces of information turn into knowledge and insight when we tell stories. Stories are how we, and the communities we make our home, convey what it is we value. And through these positive stories, we can grow our can-do narrative.

Part III:

# WELCOME HOME

# THE CHOICES WE MAKE

One evening at a dinner being held on behalf of the Harwood Institute, I recall sitting in the host's backyard in Bentonville, Arkansas. The conversation was lively and warm. At one point, the host sat up and confessed to the small group her fears about drug abuse at the local high school, where her son had recently graduated. She knew some of the kids who she felt could fall through the cracks. She worried about how, even whether, the community would help these kids.

One of the dinner guests that evening was Clifton Taulbert, a best-selling author who has written over a dozen books, including *Eight Habits of the Heart*. It's a beautiful book about his childhood growing up as an African American in the Mississippi Delta in the 1950s.

In the chapter "Brotherhood," Taulbert tells the story of different community members who took him under their wing. One was a woman who implored him never to look down in shame and humiliation when talking to others. He must always hold his head up high and look people in the eye. She said: "There's no need to count the rocks." To Taulbert, this was brotherhood in action. He writes:

> *Brotherhood is such a powerful habit of the heart that even when only one person reaches out to do right, the impact can be lifelong. If I had not encountered this habit of the heart when I was young, I could have left the South embittered and hurt. Instead I left with purpose and a plan. I could*

*not have done so without the memory of these acts of brotherhood. I needed*
*to see them practiced in front of me to believe that they could happen.*[1]

Each of us has memories that connect us to some positive teaching or experience in our lives. These memories hold for us some deeper purpose and meaning about how to make our way through life. They instruct us in the way of life. They teach us how to make certain choices.

As we talked that evening about ways we could address concerns like those Lori brought up, we each recalled positive memories from our own lives about how different people—like teachers, neighbors, grandmothers, coaches—had come to shape us to be better human beings.

Beyond recalling helpful individuals, each of us can probably also recall a time when a larger community came together to help its citizens— perhaps it was so a family would not go hungry or to help a kid go to a good public school or maybe attempts were made to close divides based on race or religion.

There's the old adage that if we don't remember our past mistakes, we repeat them. But there is something else just as powerful about memory—just as vital. Memory can tell us about how we *can* act in a positive and productive way.

Taulbert wrote that when he saw brotherhood practiced, he came to believe in its possibility. I myself have such deep memories. I learned from Mr. Rivers, Mr. Petker, and Mr. Brundidge that I had choices. For me, I could succumb to my maladies and fears or persevere and rise.

Our memories, when we pull from them, when we reignite them in ourselves, and when we share them between and among each other, help us to hear a call to step forward and engage with others. These memories unleash our potential to shape something better. They guide us to become part of something larger than ourselves. They remind us of the gifts and talents and sheer power to do good that is in each of us.

---

1   Clifton Taulbert, *Eight Habits of the Heart: Embracing the Values That Build Strong Families and Communities* (New York: Penguin, 1999), 58.

This entire book is about big and small choices we, as individuals, get to make about the kind of communities we have. It is about how we discover what we share in common and build upon it. These choices also speak to your own life: What kind of life do you want to lead and will you lean in or pull away?

To act on the concepts in this book and bring them to life requires making choices. Oftentimes, these choices can raise fears or trepidation in us. I know this; I've experienced this myself.

But what also comes with having choices is a sense of possibility and hope—that we are shapers and builders and developers of our future. Making choices enables us to take active ownership of our own lives and communities. The more intentional you are in making these choices, the more effective you will be. The greater sense of purpose and meaning you will gain in your life. To do this, you'll need to reach within and beyond yourself.

## STANDING UP

I was standing in the middle of the room among about 150 community leaders and residents from across Frederick, Maryland. We were discussing a Harwood Institute initiative called the New Patriotism Project, which sought to improve the political conduct of candidates, news media, and citizens.

At one point, I asked those in attendance to complete a personal covenant, a tool I had developed years ago for people to examine the choices they make in how they engage in their lives and their work in communities, and the expectations they hold for themselves.

Once people had completed their personal covenant, I asked if anyone wanted to share their thoughts and reflections. Among those who raised their hand was a woman in her sixties, sitting not far from me in the center of the big room. Everyone in the community seemed to know her. In fact, in our planning for the session, many people had told me that for the meeting to be credible, she had to be there. She was the dean at the local college.

When she stood up, I suspect that many of us thought she would weave some kind of insightful tale about how she had mastered making choices in her life. Then inspire the rest of us to follow her lead. We were wrong. At least I was wrong.

Instead, she stood up and said that after completing her personal covenant, she realized she was falling short of living up to her most important values. Going forward, she said, she wanted to hold herself to a higher standard. She must do better in her work in—and *with*—the community. She stood up and held herself accountable; this is what we all need to do in our lives and communities.

## THE BINDS WE'RE IN

The college dean from Frederick took one of the most difficult steps you must take in making choices. She made herself visible, present, and real. She said, in essence, "Here I am."

This reminds me of an experience I had in Winchester, the community in eastern Kentucky that is striving mightily to get beyond what's gone wrong over the years and build on the productive steps people are already taking.

When we launched our partnership there, I experienced a first in my 30 years of doing this kind of work. Two Winchester parents made the choice to pull their child out of school for three days so the entire family could attend our Public Innovators Lab to learn how to help rejuvenate their local community. The Winchester family, much like the college dean, made a choice to show up.

As we engage in our own communities, just like for these parents in Winchester, there are many choices to make along the way. They aren't always easy. They won't always be clear. They certainly don't come without challenges.

What enables us to think about these choices? What prompts us to move ahead? What holds us back? Is there any secret code to break about people making choices? Is there any special process you can go through? Are there indicators you can isolate that would make the path easier or faster or more effective?

What often is at issue when we seek to make choices is that we find ourselves in some kind of *bind*. We come to a place where questions flood us. Where doubts consume us. Where fear fills us. Where we don't exactly know the next step. These binds stymie us. Halt us. Sometimes they dispirit us.

Oftentimes, these binds trigger within us a kind of internal recording—the ones that can bring us down by playing over and over in our mind. Sometimes these personal recordings feel like they are taking over. When they do, they shape your actions, undermine your positive attitude, and shake your confidence.

There is a version of these recordings I often hear from those I work with in communities. Sometimes they focus on one bad thing, one piece of the recording; other times, it's like they're reciting the whole damn thing. Your internal struggle might sound something like this, which is what I often hear people say to me:

*I feel so small compared to what confronts me and what my community must deal with. How can I do anything about what's needed?*

*Then again, there are times when, all of a sudden, I want to take on the world. The voice whispering in my head tells me that I must do big and audacious things. Otherwise, why should I act at all?*

*Then at times I am filled with doubt. I look out over my community and worry about how change can occur. I know somehow that it doesn't happen in a straight line, but then how does it happen? The truth comes down upon me like a ton of bricks. Creating change is messy. Sometimes it's chaotic. I hate all conflict. People get emotional.*

*How can I satisfy everyone? Surely, I must try to be all things to all people. Otherwise I will fail, right?*

*But how do I prove to others I know what I am doing? Many of them think that my ideas about community are naïve, too idealistic. I know:*

*I'll get busier! I'll make a longer to-do list! I will run harder and faster!*
*Surely all this will prove my commitment to others—perhaps even to*
*myself.*

*But I am tired. On some days, I feel worn out. At times I am filled*
*with fear. Some nights I can't sleep. Some days my focus is just not clear*
*enough.*

*How can I know what makes the most sense to do? How can I cover*
*my ass? What if, by chance, I can't master everything I need to know?*
*Then what?*

*Heaven help me, I want the gold star.*

Of course, you already know there is no gold star. There is no magic
wand to wave, potion to drink, paint-by-number approach to adopt, or
mantra we can chant to elude these binds. Getting past them requires
something much deeper, more personal.

Each step along the way requires us to make choices.

## GETTING OUT OF OUR BINDS

David Moore, my colleague and good friend, once said at a Kettering
Foundation meeting that in his work in communities he finds many leaders increasingly acting as if they don't have choices. They don't see a reasonable path to take. So, they increasingly turn inward and forfeit making
the choices before them.

He attributes this further inward pull to the realization that the world
has dramatically changed around them. They feel under intense pressure
for their work and organizations or groups to be more relevant; to secure
more funding; to become more sustainable; to protect their own position
and survival. But rather than deal with these concerns, David said that
because these individuals don't believe they have choices, they get stuck.
So, they pull more and more inward. They hunker down and retreat into
what feels known and safe. In other words, they're in a bind.

People often ask me: What's the most difficult part of working with leaders and community members in helping them think about innovation and change? My response: People need to see that by making choices, they can get out of the binds they believe they're in.

The truth is that we almost always have choices. But how can we get out of feeling that we're in a bind? Surely, you cannot take on all the world's troubles on your own. Nor can you take on all the challenges in your local community. And you can't control everything that happens to you in your workplace or any kind of group.

But you do have more power than you think, and this power comes from the choices you make. One thing to consider is where can you take action—what is your sphere of influence? We all have influence in certain areas of our lives, work, and communities. What is it for you?

Also think back for a moment to many of the stories I have told. So many of them show how people found allies they could work with and rely on. Who are these people for you?

Then, you must release yourself from the burden of having to solve everything, and instead focus on what your next steps are. Once you're in action, new things inevitably open up. So, get moving.

## WHAT ABOUT *US*?

Still, there's another part of getting out of binds that I want to speak about here. It's almost a first step, a prerequisite—much like Turning Outward is when working with communities. Here's a quick story I am reminded of.

When I first started my work in Flint, one of our earliest tasks was to convene a series of community conversations. Some months after the conversations, we invited all the participants to a dinner at the old Ramada Inn, on Saginaw Street, right in the center of downtown.

That January night was particularly cold. A hard snow was falling. Like most nights after dark, the downtown streets were empty. We feared no one would show up. Then seemingly a miracle happened. One by one, people began to walk through the front doors of that old hotel, their voices loud and joyful. As people made their way into the room, they shook the cold snow off their shoulders and warmly greeted one another. Many more came than we had ever hoped for.

After some introductory comments, I asked the group a simple question: "What needs to happen for Flint to move forward?" I began to hear a common refrain in people's responses. One person said, "I think the mayor needs to do something." Then another asserted, "The United Way needs to act!" Yet another singled out an organization across town to do something. As each person spoke, the story was the same. *Other* people would need to take the lead. This is not unusual to hear from people in a community that finds itself in hard times. Nor is it uncommon to hear this refrain in most communities in our nation today.

Out of the corner of my eye, I could see a gentleman sitting to my right, who signaled that he wanted to speak. But as I looked at him, he gently nodded me off, the way people often do. So, the conversation went on. One person after another laid out the steps they believed others must take.

Eventually, after another 15 minutes of conversation, the gentleman leaned forward in his chair. This time, he nodded affirmatively for me to call on him. He was an older man. In order to stand up, he grabbed hold of the table with both hands and literally *pulled* himself out of his chair. It was as if he had willed himself to stand.

All told, he stood no more than five feet. His name, I would come to find out later, was Mr. Brooks. Before he uttered a single word, he took a long moment to look out across the room, taking in its full measure.

Then, he took a deep breath, and said these few words: "What about us? What are we in this room going to do? What about us?"

## BEING INTENTIONAL

Whether you are an executive of an organization, a staff member or board member; whether you are a community resident; whether you are clergy or a lay leader of a congregation or one of its members. Whoever you may be: What about us? What are you going to do to step forward?

Our dinner host in Bentonville had wondered aloud about whether her community would support kids who were falling into the grip of drugs and related problems. Clifton Taulbert reminded us that everyone holds memories about how an individual, or some collection of others, helped us to improve our lives and the life of our community. He was in essence responding to our host's call: Many times we know what we need to do, but we just need to remember what we know.

You and I find ourselves in a series of binds when we try to act on what we know. These binds come in many forms. They are real. They stymie the best of our intentions. At times, they short-circuit our memory. They strike fear in us, generate trepidation, raise questions, and worry us over what others will think of our efforts. It's hard to remember things when we feel stress and worry.

But then along come people like the college dean in Frederick. She reminds us that we can remember what we aspire to do and who we aspire to be. She teaches us not to fall prey to the fears and trepidations and self-doubts that bind us. In standing up that day, she told us that we can and must—that we will—overcome these binds when we rediscover what we hold to be most valuable in our lives and in our communities. Mr. Brooks leaves us with the most potent question of all: What about us?

My intent is not to implore you to have more confidence in yourself to overcome the binds you experience in your daily life and work. Those would be empty words. They'd fail to address a real challenge you face. I want to help you find a better and stronger way to make choices. When you do, you can fortify your confidence, not based on empty rhetoric, but on something more reliable, durable, and time-tested.

Yes, to get out of binds you can think about your sphere of influence, who your allies are, and what next steps you can take. But even closer to the heart of the matter is this: To make any good choice—whether it deals with community or public life or our own personal lives—requires you to be intentional. When you become more intentional, you engage in acts of discernment—sorting through what you confront, its different meanings and possibilities. You develop a greater wherewithal to make more explicit choices.

By being more intentional, you see and articulate the reasons for your choices. You develop ways to define and even defend them. You set out a course of action to follow and know that it's possible to change your course along the way as you learn more.

This is what grows and expands and deepens your confidence. Such confidence is not simply announced or declared. Your confidence is something you *create*, over time, through your ability to be intentional about the choices you make.

I am personally moved by the following definition of intentionality, which comes in two parts.

Being intentional involves what I think of as "wakefulness." I love this word. Take a moment to consider its meaning and the potential for your own engagement.

Wakefulness suggests that you are alert. You come to the world awake. In this way, your eyes are wide open. You heart is enlarged. You are open to see and hear more of what's around you and on a deeper level. In being wakeful, you stand ready to engage, to be *with* others.

The notion of wakefulness stands in direct contrast to current negative conditions in society, such as the polarization in our public discourse, the blinders so many of us put on so we won't need to worry about certain issues or matters, and the great lengths some of us go to take in only news and information that confirm what we already know or believe.

Wakefulness is the opposite of inwardness. It is about being present, about being *real*, especially for those things we do not like, that make us uncomfortable, or may be hurtful to us. To be wakeful is to be turned outward.

The companion to wakefulness is "moral accountability." This suggests that your actions do not come free of strings attached. There are consequences and ramifications to what you do. Before you say this sounds like a new constraint or something negative, I ask you to consider that what I am really saying is that you have power.

Embedded within the notion of moral accountability is that while you cannot control everything in your life, you do exercise power over much of what you do. Not absolute power, of course. But enough power that you can see the potential for action. In that potential, you hold a responsibility to account for what you do. You must recognize and grab hold of the potential you have to positively or negatively impact people and your surroundings.

One reason why I cherish the notion of moral accountability is that when we embrace it, we begin to see our own potential can shape the world around us. We become actors, not mere spectators; shapers, not mere bystanders; builders, not mere complainers or claimants. Being intentional boils down to what we choose to make of ourselves. What we choose to do with ourselves.

How will we bring our full selves to be in relationships with others? How will we lean in to our lives? How will we create shared lives? In this spirit, when I speak of being intentional, my goal is not for you to adopt wholesale my ideas or anyone else's. That would be the very antithesis of what I am asking you to do.

Instead, the process of deepening your own intentionality requires you to take ownership of the choices that stand before you. You must find and declare your own sense of purpose. You must choose your own course of engagement with those around you.

What I am asking you to do is to seize your intrinsic power and step forward.

# I THOUGHT MY SOUL
# WOULD RISE AND FLY

I was once asked by my good friend Deborah Kohler, then pastor of Woodside Church in Flint, to preach one Sunday morning. I was thrilled at the opportunity. We agreed I'd select two readings from Scripture to frame the service and my sermon.

After days of thinking about what to choose, I settled on two passages. The ones I had initially reached for.

The first text was Matthew 5:15–16, the well-known verse that tells each of us to take our light out from under the bushel to shine it before all people. This text is especially meaningful for those of us who believe we must value the human spark and tap our innate capabilities to repair breaches in society. At the time, in Flint, as I have said, many people had retreated from one another. Their faith in government, in themselves, and in each other had eroded. Fear and despair abounded. The text resonated deeply that Sunday morning—as it might in most communities.

The second reading was Psalm 27. I remember the first time I read this psalm many years ago. It was during a period of my life when my work was especially difficult. People were telling me that what I wanted to do—what I've described in part in this book—couldn't work, wouldn't work. They kept telling me that I should give up on my dreams and go do something else. When I first read Psalm 27, it comforted me. It also fed me.

Psalm 27 talks about the enemies that will encamp against us as we seek to live a life of purpose and meaning. A portion of it reads:

*Though an army shall encamp against me, my heart will not be afraid;*
*Though war should be waged against me, I shall still be confident.*

On that Sunday morning at Woodside Church, some people were surprised at my selection of this second text. The first one made total sense to them. They had heard me speak many times about the power of individuals to create a sense of possibility and hope. How each of us must reach within ourselves and beyond ourselves to create the kinds of communities, society, and lives we seek.

But Psalm 27 was a different story. It had a much harder edge to it. The very words that make it up—*army, encamp, war, wage, against me*—seemed so unlike what people had become used to hearing me speak about. Was I picking a fight with someone from the pulpit? Was I contradicting the very messages I had often given? Was I encouraging people to cross a line they thought I had drawn concerning human dignity and decency?

After the service, Pete Hutchison, a long-time Flint resident and activist who I had come to know and trust, indeed someone I had come to love, came and stood next to me. He said, "There are less combative portions of Scripture than Psalm 27." He suggested that my future talks might benefit from one of these other passages.

As Pete spoke, I stood there in silence, wondering to myself, *Should I have used a different reading? Have I crossed a line?* After a moment of reflection, I responded to Pete, "No, this passage captures exactly what I wanted to say."

On that Sunday, the topic of my sermon was what it means to show your face and step forward amid tough conditions in our lives and communities. Where one's efforts run against prevailing forces. Where you might be criticized for sticking your neck out. Where it would be far easier to keep your head down. My point that morning was we ought not to hide despite any fears we have about stepping forward. No matter how big the challenges are before the community—and before us. Each of us must find our light under the bushel and make it visible for all to see. Then we must follow our own light and inspire others to find theirs. Only then can we find what we share in common and build upon it.

But, truth be told, these notions will not be enough by themselves. Alone, they will not produce the sense of possibility and hope we yearn for. Enemies—naysayers, critics, opponents, and others—will encamp against us. Seek to pull us down. Attempt to divert our attention. Try to push us off our path. Tell us our aspirations are unrealistic and unachievable. "Just give in!" they'll shout.

We must not shy away from these enemies or pretend they don't exist. We can't simply wish them away or believe they'll magically disappear. Our task is to find ways to keep on our path. We must show our face.

## A STAKE IN THE GROUND

On this journey we're on, you will need courage. Sadly, politicians, community leaders, and self-help gurus often use this word as a self-anointed badge of honor. If only you repeat it enough times, you'll embody it. If only you wish for it hard enough, somehow it becomes emblazed on your heart. By shouting it loudly enough, it seeps into your very being.

This idea of courage is an attempt to embolden, even inflate, our sense of self-worth. At times, we strut about with bravado. We beat our breasts. We raise our voices. But it's hollow bravery and rhetoric. It only leads us to a false sense of power and more wrong turns. It prompts us to believe we can say and do what we wish, without consequence.

This hollowed-out courage steals from us opportunities for genuine engagement and progress. And it becomes a way to keep our distance from others. We stand apart. We pursue our own course without having to take seriously other people and their views. We think we are always in the right.

The courage necessary to reimagine the opportunity before us, and then to turn outward, asks something different of us. This courage underpins the very first act I asked you to consider at the start of this book: Step forward and say, "Here I am."

Taking this single step requires nothing less than being present in the world. We are by definition connected to others. It necessitates that we assume ownership over what we say and do. This is the courage that allows us to engage with others—to be *with* others. It gives us the strength and wherewithal to enter into real give and take with others, and makes us brave enough to face hard situations and work things out with others.

In exercising this courage, we can temper our fear of others and not run the other way. Or merely seek to run harder or faster as a substitute for being purposeful. Others can see and hear us. We can be in relationship with them.

When I worked with Stacey Stewart, when she was US president of United Way Worldwide, she said whenever she could to local United Way leaders that everyone in your community should know what you stand for. Courage is about placing a stake in the ground. "This is what I believe. This is what I will do." Such courage is rooted in the acknowledgment that all the planning and groundwork in the world will take us only so far, for so long. At some point, we must declare what we are for.

Such courage calls upon us to understand the truth as best we can, to face reality, and to not get lost in utopian visions and plans, which cloud it. There is no time to get sidetracked by busyness and inward-looking activities.

Courage is required to make choices. And it takes being intentional about them.

No doubt this courage will give rise to fear within you. Facing reality can be difficult. Being present is often hard. Bringing our full selves to the tasks at hand—well, sometimes it's easier to go halfway. Making choices involves trade-offs. You cannot be all things to all people.

I am asking you to embrace your commitments, not sidestep them. Summon the ability to move beyond the superficial and the trivial. Authentically engage with others. I am asking you to show your face.

## BEING OPEN

Courage alone is not enough. It must never be exercised in isolation. On its own, it can easily lead us to hubris. So, there is a second thing you will need along with courage to make your way forward: humility.

For me, humility is one of the most beautiful notions there is. It is intrinsic to what makes us human—reminding us of our own vulnerabilities, fears, the sense that we are not whole without others.

Too often when people make attempts at humility, it's mere lip service. A kind of feigned attempt filled with false modesty and practiced posturing. Such humility is often invoked right before one makes use of bravado.

Humility is the flip side of courage, the *necessary* flip side. Without the active presence of humility, we cannot exercise true courage. When each of us seeks to place a stake in the ground, it takes humility to know where to place it. For humility tells us that we alone do not hold all the answers. We must open ourselves up to listen to others. To take in what they say. Consider its meaning. Often when we do, we discover the need to alter our own ideas and answers.

Courage is tempered by humility.

Sometimes the only way to understand ourselves is to sit silently and listen to others. It is through other people's words and emotions that we make sense of who we are and what we think and feel. These discoveries come about only when we have the humility to see and hear others. Only when we open ourselves up to others.

With humility, we know that the stake we once placed in the ground will need to be picked up and moved. Nothing involving people and communities ever remains static. They are forever changing and evolving. And so we must change with them. It takes humility to remain open, even in our dogged pursuit of our most treasured goals.

And this stake you must pick up, you might have to pick it up in public, and that takes humility. When humility is present we understand that making mid-course corrections is not a weakness but a true strength. We are ready to deal with change and to engage ambiguity where we find it.

I am reminded of something Suzie Armstrong, who at the time served as vice president of the Interfaith Alliance in Washington, DC, once said to me. In reflecting on her personal efforts to fulfill her organization's advocacy work, she said, "I realize I don't have enough humility. As an advocate, it's hard to stop and listen."

This was many years ago. I still have deep admiration for Suzie's honesty and vulnerability all these years later. When each of us is able to exercise humility and engage with others, our boundaries enlarge. We discover new things. We learn. We grow.

Without humility, we remain potentially separated from one another, rather than come together. We close down our boundaries, rather than open them. We constrict and narrow our view and understanding of others, rather than expand them.

It is nearly impossible to be open—to hear, understand, feel—without a good measure of humility. St. Augustine once said, "There is then, strange to say, something in humility, which raises the heart upwards." When I speak of such humility, I am not asking you to embrace false modesty or relinquish the convictions of your beliefs. The humility I have in mind is the prerequisite to opening yourself up to the world, while understanding that you must maintain the values and beliefs close to your heart.

Humility liberates us to be with others, enabling us to connect with others, while never losing sight of our self.

You should know that when you need courage and humility most is when they can seem least accessible to you. At these times, it can seem hard to locate either courage or humility and put them into action. Yet it is in these very moments that you must actively search for them. Even in your doubts, you must remind yourself of the need for courage and humility and seek to make good use of them. That only happens when you know their importance and keep them close to you in your daily life.

## RELEASE YOURSELF AND RISE

When God called out to Moses at the burning bush, he said, "I will bring you out from under the burden of the Egyptians." I am told that in Hebrew, one interpretation of the word "burden" is not to shoulder some great pain or imposition. But there's another meaning: resignation or acceptance.

So the charge to Moses was that God would lead the Israelites to freedom but that they must no longer accept their plight. To reject the destiny they thought they had been handed. Stand up and do something. Isn't this the situation we face today?

The old slave song "Free at Last" tells us a similar story. In the song's second verse, you'll find some of the most moving words I've ever heard: "I thought my soul would rise and fly."

Their words were rooted in hope, perhaps even expectation, about what might come. Somehow, they believed tomorrow would be different from today. They chose not to be resigned to their horrific plight. Their singing was a declaration of their intentions to move beyond their immediate condition. A refusal—they would not accept the burden of oppression.

The slaves showed us what is humanly possible, even under their unimaginable circumstances. They remind us of our aspirations. That we hold aspirations for what we yearn for, but are not yet within our grasp.

If we are to improve our shared lives, then we must release ourselves from our resignation that things must be the way they are today. We can declare they can be better. We can be better. We must let our light shine, knowing that others may resist our efforts. With courage and humility, we can step forward.

# THE REDISCOVERY

A number of years ago, my son, Jonathan, and I took a walk together along the Camino de Santiago, the old Christian pilgrimage in Spain. The main route ends at the far northwestern tip of the country, at the cathedral of Santiago de Compostela.

The pilgrimage actually has many routes. There is a route that starts in southwestern France and then makes its way into Spain. Another begins in Portugal, from the south of Spain, and moves north. A third is simply a straight line that comes from the far eastern point of Spain, spanning the entire northern tier of the country. There are others, too.

Depending upon the route one takes, the trek can be upwards of 500 miles. People spend months walking it. Jonathan and I had time to walk about 150 miles over about two weeks. It was long enough to find a rhythm that worked for both of us. Each day, we'd rise early, walk together during the morning hours, and then each afternoon walk on our own. Eventually, we'd come back together in the late afternoon and walk well into the evening. Then we'd search for a place to eat and sleep.

We found ourselves deep in conversation each day—including topics such as what does it mean to truly listen, what is a vocation and calling, how does one pursue excellence in their craft, how do we make choices in our lives. This was one of the most beautiful experiences of my life.

When I returned home, people would ask me how I liked the trip and what I took away from it. After many failed attempts to answer their questions, I could hear myself starting to say the same thing to different people: It's not that I discovered anything new on the trip. It's what I rediscovered.

I found that what matters most in life—those things that we are most in search of—is often right in front of us. If only we are able to see them. If only we will value them, embrace them, and make them real in our lives again.

In many ways, a rediscovery is what sits at the heart of this book. It is about what each of us already know but sometimes misplace or forget. About those things that get caked over or pushed aside in the rush of our daily lives. It is about losing ourselves in inwardness and making the wrong turns.

This rediscovery requires that you stop long enough to remember.

Remember, that we must reject resigning ourselves to the fears and frustrations that trouble us today.

Remember, that we each have a choice in whether to step forward, make ourselves visible, and be present and engage with others. To declare, "Here I am."

Remember, that we have the innate capabilities to take a more hopeful path, where we focus on our shared lives and build together.

Remember, that you can bring greater purpose and meaning back into our own life when you take this more hopeful path.

Let us rediscover what we already know.

Together, we are the creators of the communities and lives we yearn for.

# ABOUT THE AUTHOR

 Richard C. Harwood is an innovator, writer, and speaker. For over three decades, he has devoted his career to revitalizing the nation's hardest-hit communities, transforming the world's largest organizations, and reconnecting institutions to society.

He has developed a philosophy and practice of how communities and society can solve common problems, create a culture of shared responsibility, and deepen civic faith. The Harwood practice of Turning Outward has spread to all 50 US states and is being used in 40 countries. His experience working on the ground to build capacity and coalitions for change gives him a unique, powerful insight on bridging divides and creating resilient communities.

Dedicated to providing a trusted civic voice, Rich's leadership has guided people in communities to see and hear one another, afford dignity to every individual, and find ways to do common work. In Newtown, Connecticut, after the massacre at Sandy Hook Elementary School, Rich led the process for the community to collectively decide the fate of the school building.

An inspiring, sought-after speaker, Rich regularly keynotes major conferences and events. He has written several books, scores of articles and groundbreaking reports, and frequently appears on national media. He is the founder and president of The Harwood Institute for Public Innovation, located in Bethesda, Maryland.

More information about Rich Harwood can be found at www.the harwoodinstitute.org. You can connect with Rich Harwood on Facebook, Twitter, and LinkedIn.